The miniature dress group showing the remarkable series of awards won by Major General Dudley Johnson (1884–1975). He won his Victoria Cross with the 2nd Royal Sussex on 4th November 1918 in the attack over the Sambre Canal. As can be seen, he was also a Companion of the Order of the Bath (CB) and held the Distinguished Service Order and bar and Military Cross – representing a truly outstanding record of gallantry and service.

The
Victoria Cross

Peter Duckers

A Shire

Published in 2005 by Shire Publications Ltd,
Cromwell House, Church Street, Princes Risborough,
Buckinghamshire HP27 9AA, UK.
(Website: www.shirebooks.co.uk)

Copyright © 2005 by Peter Duckers.
First published 2005.
Shire Album 447. ISBN-10: 0 7478 0635 7;
ISBN-13: 978 0 7478 0635 7.
Peter Duckers is hereby identified as the author of this
work in accordance with Section 77 of the Copyright,
Designs and Patents Act 1988.

British Library Cataloguing in Publication Data:
Duckers, Peter
The Victoria Cross. – (Shire album; 447)
1. Victoria Cross 2. Victoria Cross – History
3. Heroes – Great Britain – Biography
4. Great Britain – History, Military
5. Great Britain – Armed Forces – Medals, badges,
decorations, etc
I. Title 355.1'342'0941
ISBN-10: 0 7478 0635 7.

Cover: *The Victoria Cross (obverse). The background shows Lance Corporal Michael O'Leary of the Irish Guards attacking the German lines at Cuinchy on 1st February 1915, an act of valour for which he was awarded the Victoria Cross (see page 24).*

ACKNOWLEDGEMENTS
The author would like to thank the following for permission to reproduce items and illustrations used in this book on the pages indicated: the auction houses Dix, Noonan, Webb (pages 21, 22 bottom, 23, 26, 33, 56, 69); Morton & Eden (pages 14 top, 16 bottom, 30 bottom); and Spink (pages 25, 38, 40, 42, 44); also *Medal News* (page 51 bottom), Mr C. N. Mitchell (pages 54 bottom left, 61 bottom) and Mr M. Cashmore (page 6). The illustration of the prototype Victoria Cross (page 13 top) is reproduced by kind permission of the National Army Museum. Other items and illustrations are from the Shropshire Regimental Museum or the author's own collection.

Printed in Malta by Gutenberg Press Limited, Gudja Road, Tarxien PLA 19, Malta

Contents

The origins of gallantry awards

The idea of rewarding gallantry in battle goes back to the earliest days of organised states. Exactly *how* such gallantry has been rewarded varies from country to country and era to era but includes grants of land or money, advancements in rank or social status, presentation weapons or jewels, and increased pay. The idea of conferring a wearable badge as a visible reward for gallantry seems to date back to the ancient Greeks and, from them, to the Romans. The Roman army established a standardised system of badges that soldiers could wear on their uniform, images of which sometimes appear on their gravestones.

In Britain, the earliest gallantry medals date to the Civil Wars of 1642–51. Examples are the gold medals given by Charles I to Sir Robert Welch and John Smith for gallantry exhibited in October 1642 at Edgehill, where they saved the King's Colours. These are probably the earliest British medals for bravery in battle. In May 1643, in court in Oxford, the King decreed that medals 'be delivered to wear on the breast of every man who shall be certified under the hands of their commanders-in-chief to have done faithful service in the forlorn hope', and others were granted by commanders such as the Earl of Manchester and Sir Thomas Fairfax.

Such military rewards were very much personal or *ad hoc* issues, given by high-ranking leaders to deserving soldiers, and were not

A military reward of the Civil War period, in this case presented by Sir Thomas Fairfax. Badges such as this were conferred by the King and by leading commanders, but the circumstances and conditions of the award are not known. Some were undoubtedly given for gallantry in battle, but others were for meritorious service.

The Commonwealth Naval Medal, instituted in 1649 to reward action against Royalist ships off the coast of Holland. It was intended that there would be future issues of the medal for 'extraordinary service' at sea. Here we have the first hint of a national system of rewards for distinguished service.

Above: A Naval Reward of the reign of Charles II. These were sparingly granted for gallantry in action against the Dutch, although it is not clear what their conditions of award actually were. This embryonic system did not, however, develop into a standardised structure for rewarding gallantry during the eighteenth century.

part of a regulated national system – their designs, sizes and metals varied and there was no official procedure for award. The first hint of an organised system appeared in the 1650s during the Commonwealth, when naval rewards were issued for gallantry in the Dutch Wars. However, although these continued into the reigns of Charles II and William III, an official system of gallantry awards did not develop and in the eighteenth century there was a return to the *ad hoc* system of individual medals produced as and when required. By the end

An example of a regimental award of the Napoleonic Wars. This is the Sergeants' Badge of the 2–53rd awarded by the Colonel of the regiment to fifteen sergeants for gallantry in the Peninsular War. This one, for Salamanca in 1812, was conferred upon Sergeant Thomas Cox. Such unofficial awards could be worn in uniform and seem to have been highly regarded.

Since there was no national system of gallantry awards, unofficial medals were issued well into the nineteenth century. This regimental example was awarded to a British soldier of the Bombay Artillery 'for eminent service in the field' in 1842 during the First Afghan War.

of the century gallantry medals were being awarded by regimental commanders, wealthy individuals and even societies. During the French Wars of 1793–1815, for example, an extensive range of unofficial medals and badges for bravery appeared, many paid for by regimental commanders to reward the gallantry of their own men. In an era when the giving of any sort of medal – even for simple campaign service – was not the norm, the issue of unofficial types continued well into the nineteenth century. A well-known example is Sir Harry Smith's Medal for Gallantry, given in 1851 to about thirty men of the Cape Mounted Rifles for bravery on campaign in South Africa.

The introduction of a standardised system of reward

It might be argued that the Army Gold Crosses and Gold Medals and their naval equivalents instituted for officers during the French Wars of 1793–1815 were the first official British awards for gallantry. They were sparingly awarded and some were indeed granted for bravery 'under fire'. However, the issue is not clear-cut – many were given for 'distinguished service' or leadership rather than for specifically gallant conduct. Similarly, the extension of the Order of the Bath at Companion level (CB) in 1815 created an award that *could* be given to officers for bravery in action but came to be conferred for long and distinguished service rather than for a single act of gallantry. In any case, these were for officers only and there was no official equivalent to reward other ranks in any of the forces – Army, Navy or Marines. Equally, other rewards, such as mentions in dispatches for gallant conduct, were rarely made for other ranks and the system of conferring rank advances by brevet was restricted to officers.

A Companion's Breast Badge of the Order of the Bath (CB). Introduced in 1815, initially to reward officers for services in the recent French Wars, some were undoubtedly conferred for bravery in action. But they came to be rewards for long and distinguished service rather than for bravery in a single action or campaign.

Above: *The Army Gold Cross, instituted in 1813. They followed the Navy and Army Gold Medals as officers' rewards for 'conspicuous services' during the French Wars. They were not, however, purely or simply gallantry awards and were discontinued in 1815.*

*The Indian Order of Merit (IOM) –
a Third Class breast badge of
1837–1912. The first regularised
award for gallantry was the IOM,
whose three classes were introduced
by the East India Company in 1837.
They remained in use, with modi-
fications, until Indian independence
in 1947.*

It was the East India Company that led the way in the general
introduction of medals. It began to issue standardised campaign
medals for its Indian soldiers from the 1780s onwards and in 1837
instituted the Order of Merit – the first regularised medal for
gallantry in battle. The Order had three classes and a soldier
technically had to be in possession of a lower grade before
promotion to a higher class. Before the introduction of the Indian
Distinguished Service Medal in 1907 and the extension of the
Victoria Cross to Indians in 1911, the Indian Order of Merit (IOM)
was the only medal for gallantry available to Indian soldiers. It
carried increased rates of pay and pension as additional rewards
and was highly regarded.

The impact of the Russian War, 1854–6

Only during the Russian War of 1854–6 was the British government finally roused into the establishment of a standardised system of gallantry awards. What is commonly known as the 'Crimean War' – after the campaign waged in the Crimea by Britain and her allies – was the first major conflict to be extensively covered by war correspondents and reported in detail in the British press. The most famous example is William Howard Russell of *The Times*, whose comprehensive and damning reports brought home graphically to the reading public the gallantry and suffering of British soldiers and sailors. Though often badly led, poorly equipped and suffering terrible privations, they nevertheless carried out feats of remarkable gallantry. As the war dragged on, with famous incidents such as the Charge of the Light Brigade, the Thin Red

A contemporary print of the Battle of Inkermann on 5th November 1854 during the Crimean War. It was not simply the fact of close combat such as this but its widespread reporting in the press that made the reading public more aware of the gallantry and exertions of British forces.

The Distinguished Conduct Medal, (DCM) showing the 'trophy of arms' obverse used on Victorian issues. Instituted in 1854 as a direct result of the Crimean War, it remained in use until 1993, when it was abolished along with other medals (but not crosses) for gallantry following a sweeping reform of the honours system.

Line at Balaklava and the horrors of the Russian winter in the trenches before Sebastopol, there were growing calls for some form of official recognition of the bravery of British forces before the enemy.

As a result, two new gallantry awards were instituted during the Crimean War. The Distinguished Conduct Medal (DCM) was established by Royal Warrant of 4th December 1854 and first awarded in 1855. It could be conferred upon 'other ranks' of the British Army but not on officers. The Conspicuous Gallantry Medal (CGM), established by Order in Council of 13th September 1855, was awarded to non-officer ranks of the Royal Navy and Royal Marines and was their equivalent of the DCM. Only ten were originally awarded and the medal was re-instituted in July 1874.

The creation of the Victoria Cross

Even the Distinguished Conduct Medal and the Conspicuous Gallantry Medal were not deemed sufficient to answer the need for appropriate recognition of services. Constant reference in *The Times* and other newspapers to the gallantry of British troops in the Crimea spurred on demands for a distinctive award that would be available to all ranks and all services.

The first practical move towards the establishment of the Victoria Cross was made by the Member of Parliament for Bath, Captain G. T. Scobell (1785–1869). On 19th December 1854 he moved in the Commons for the creation of 'an "Order of Merit" to be bestowed upon persons serving in the Army or Navy for distinguished and prominent personal gallantry' (*Hansard*, December 1854). Matters then moved quickly. The Secretary for War, the Duke of Newcastle, put the idea before Prince Albert in January 1855 and from then on both the Prince Consort and Queen Victoria played a leading role in establishing the new 'Order'.

Work began on the drawing up of the original Warrant – the conditions governing the award of the medal – and on the design

The Charge of the Light Brigade at Balaklava on 25th October 1854. The fighting in the Crimean War (1854–6) was the first to be reported in detail by war correspondents and captured by photographers. They helped to perpetuate the famous incidents – and myths – of the war and to bring home to the public the reality of the situation faced by British forces.

of the medal itself. Enquiries were made about foreign Orders that might be comparable, for example the Spanish Order of St Ferdinand and the Austrian Order of Maria Theresa, but in the end the idea of an 'Order', suggesting a graded confraternity of high-ranking persons including the sovereign, was abandoned. The Queen herself favoured a standardised 'decoration' available in one grade only and open to all ranks – and perhaps we should recall that at this time Britain was fighting as an ally of France, whose Legion of Honour (instituted in 1802) provided an example of such a decoration.

Various names for the award were put before the Queen, examples being the 'Military Order of Victoria' and the 'Order of Valour', but it was quickly altered (apparently by Prince Albert) to 'Victoria Cross'. Mottoes were also considered – from *Mors aut Victoria* ('Death or Victory') to *The Reward of Valour* (which coincidentally or not was the motto of the existing Indian Order of Merit), *Reward of Bravery*, *For Bravery* and *To the Brave*. In the end it was the Queen herself who proposed the simple motto *For Valour*. Queen Victoria was equally involved in choosing the metal – copper, brass, steel and bronze all being proposed – and favoured bronze (or 'gun-metal'), artificially toned to darken it and give highlights to the raised parts of the design when polished.

The design of the Victoria Cross, which is similar in shape to the Army Gold Cross of 1813–15 (see page 7), seems to have been produced 'in house' by Hancocks, the London jewellers who have always cast the medal. It may have been the work of H. M. Armstead, one of their principal designers at that time. Initially, each Cross cost the Government £1, with an additional three shillings (15p) for the engraved personal details.

The Royal Warrant instituting the award, which was made retrospective to 1st August 1854, was signed by the Queen on 29th January 1856 and announced in *The London Gazette* on 5th February. But because of the detailed work required to finalise the design and produce the medal, another year passed before any were ready for issue. The first awards were published in *The London Gazette* on 24th February 1857 and the first presentations took place in Hyde Park on 26th June, when the Queen personally presented sixty-two Victoria Crosses for actions in the Baltic, the Sea of Azoff and the Crimea.

The whole concept of the Victoria Cross was remarkably democratic for its day – it conferred no title or rank, it existed in only one form and grade for all recipients (unlike the various 'classes' of the Orders) and, most unusually, the new medal was open on the same terms to all ranks and full-time services – Army, Navy and Marines. At first, however, it could not be awarded posthumously (see page 61).

The Victoria Cross, obverse.

The prototype Victoria Cross, made by Hancocks and presented to Queen Victoria for her approval, which it received on 3rd March 1856. (NAM 6310-59)

Not surprisingly, there was a great deal of public and press interest in the new award, and at the first presentation in Hyde Park the newly decorated recipients were mobbed by spectators anxious for a glimpse of the medal. Some elements of the press were less than enthusiastic; the reporter of *The Times* commented:

> Than the Cross of Valour nothing could be more plain and homely, not to say coarse-looking. It is a very small Maltese cross, formed from the gun-metal of ordnance captured at Sebastopol. In the centre is a small crown and lion, with which latter's natural proportions of mane and tail the cutting of the cross much interferes. Below these is a small scroll (which shortens three arms of the cross and is utterly out of

The first Victoria Cross presentation in Hyde Park on 26th June 1857, as depicted in The Illustrated London News. The Queen, somewhat strangely, remained mounted on horseback throughout the entire ceremony.

The medals of Private John Pearson, 8th Hussars. His group comprises the Victoria Cross, the Crimea medal with clasps 'Balaklava' and 'Sebastopol', the Indian Mutiny medal with clasp 'Central India', the Meritorious Service Medal and the Turkish medal for the Crimea. Pearson, who had already ridden in the Charge of the Light Brigade at Balaklava, was one of four regimental VCs chosen by ballot (see page 60) after the Battle of Gwalior on 17th June 1858 during the Central India campaign. Note the unofficial decorative brooches from which the medals are worn.

keeping with the upper portions) bearing the words 'For Valour' ... the whole cross is, after all, poor looking and mean in the extreme.

But *The Times* missed the point. The fact that it was simply, to use one current phrase, 'tuppence worth of bronze' was intentional – it deliberately eschewed the glamour of gold and enamels as in the grand Orders. It is a plain badge that declares the wearer's bravery in action; it is the gallantry represented by the award that matters, not its status as a jewel or adornment. And despite initially adverse comments, the Victoria Cross has stood the test of time and remains unaltered in design.

An extract from 'The London Gazette', 25th February 1862, with the citation for an award of the Victoria Cross. Shown is the award to Lieutenant William Waller, 25th Bombay Light Infantry (1827–77), for his gallantry in the attack on the fortress of Gwalior on 20th June 1858 – nearly four years earlier! All awards of the Victoria Cross are published in 'The London Gazette', an official government publication, and/or its colonial counterparts such as 'The Gazette of India'.

| 25th Bombay Light Infantry | Lieutenant William Francis Frederick Waller

Date of Act of Bravery, June 20th, 1858. | For great gallantry at the capture by storm of the fortress of Gwalior, on the 20th June, 1858. He and Lieutenant Rose, who was killed, were the only Europeans present, and, with a mere handful of men, they attacked the fortress, climbed on the roof of a house, shot the gunners opposed to them, carried all before them, and took the fort, killing every man in it, |

Description of the Victoria Cross

The medal is in the form of a cross pattée (not, as is often claimed, a Maltese cross) and depicts on the obverse a lion *statant gardant* over the royal crown, around which is a scroll bearing the words *For Valour*. It is cast in bronze and then chased and finished by hand before being chemically treated to darken it. The reverse of the Cross is plain, except for a central roundel in which is engraved the date of the action for which the medal is awarded.

The Cross is suspended from its ribbon by means of a straight bar, decorated with laurel leaves, which is joined to the medal by a small 'V' and a single circular metal link. The reverse of the suspension bar is engraved in capital letters with the details of the recipient – number, rank, name and unit.

Variations in the hand-finishing and depth of chemical colouring mean that each Victoria Cross is slightly different. The medal is 1.37 inches (35 mm) wide and 1.6 inches (41 mm) high and, with its suspension bar, weighs approximately 0.87 troy ounces. By tradition, the metal is taken from Russian guns captured during the Siege of Sebastopol (1854–6), though it is believed that gun-

The reverse of the Victoria Cross, showing the typical naming details. The engraving style naturally varies from era to era, but the general presentation of personal detail is the same. The recipient's number, rank, name and unit are engraved in block capitals on the back of the suspension bar and the date of the incident or incidents for which the medal was awarded is engraved in the central roundel on the reverse (see also page 63 on Parkes).

Right: *The remaining block of bronze or 'gun-metal' from which any future Victoria Crosses would be cast. It was taken from the breech of a Russian gun captured at Sebastopol (the traditional source of metal for the Victoria Cross).*

The miniature Victoria Cross emblem. These are borne on the Victoria Cross ribbon when a ribbon alone is being worn. A winner of the Victoria Cross and bar would wear two miniature emblems.

metal from other sources was used for some Victoria Crosses awarded during the two world wars. The piece of metal from which any future Crosses would be taken is held at the Defence Storage and Distribution Centre (DFDS) in Donnington, Shropshire.

The ribbon for Army awards is described as 'red' in the Warrant, though it is often referred to as 'crimson'; it is 1.5 inches (38 mm) wide. Originally the Victoria Cross ribbon for Royal Navy and Royal Marine recipients was dark blue but in 1918, at the time of the formation of the Royal Air Force, the ribbon was standardised to crimson for all services.

Since 1918, when the recipient wears the ribbon alone a miniature Victoria Cross is displayed in the centre of the piece of ribbon, the award of a bar to the Cross being indicated by the wearing of two miniature emblems.

In early times there was no officially prescribed order of wear for decorations and medals. In this contemporary photograph Private Pearson, 8th Hussars (see page 14), wears his Victoria Cross in the middle of his group of campaign medals. Not until 1902 was it decreed that the Victoria Cross should be worn before all other decorations and medals.

A formal presentation of the Victoria Cross: Sergeant Harold Whitfield, Shropshire Yeomanry and 10th King's Shropshire Light Infantry, receives the Cross from King George V in Leeds in May 1918. Whenever possible, the Victoria Cross is personally presented by the monarch in the most formal of ceremonies. However, when this was not practicable – in times of war or in the case of great distance (as with imperial awards) – a local commander of high rank or civic dignitary, such as a governor or the Viceroy, would present the award.

In early Victorian times, the position of wear of decorations and medals relative to each other was not formally prescribed and photographs show men wearing their awards in a variety of decorative ways. Only in 1881 did Queen's Regulations lay down the position of the Victoria Cross when worn with other awards and not until 1902 was it directed (by King Edward VII) that it must be worn before all other decorations and medals. Dress Regulations of 1904 reflected that change.

Major changes to Victoria Cross Warrants

Royal Warrant of 29th January 1856 laid down the initial terms of award in fifteen clauses.

The Victoria Cross was extended to the forces of the East India Company in October 1857 – but not to its native troops, who had to wait until 1911.

Royal Warrant of 10th August 1858 allowed for the award of the Victoria Cross under 'circumstances of extreme danger', not necessarily in the face of an enemy.

Royal Warrant of 1st January 1867 extended the Victoria Cross to 'local forces' serving alongside Imperial troops – for example to members of the New Zealand Militias serving in the Maori Wars, one of whom was the first recipient under this new clause.

Royal Warrant of 23rd April 1881 effectively revoked the clause allowing for award in circumstances not 'in the presence of the enemy'. The Victoria Cross was extended to the auxiliary and reserve forces of the Army and Navy.

Royal Warrant of 6th August 1881 extended eligibility to the Indian Ecclesiastical Departments (i.e. civil chaplains of the IED when serving with the forces).

Royal Warrant of 21st October 1911 extended the award of the Victoria Cross to the native personnel of the Indian Army and laid down pension payments to be associated with it.

Royal Warrant of 22nd May 1920 made specific provision for posthumous awards to be made. The Victoria Cross was extended to the newly formed Royal Air Force, to the Merchant Navy, to women

The New Zealand Cross. This 'colonial VC' was instituted by the New Zealand authorities in 1869 to reward soldiers of the local militias who had borne the brunt of the fighting during the Maori Wars (1860–70). The authorities in Britain reacted sternly to the unilateral creation of such a decoration – the monarch being the sole 'fount of honour' – and only twenty-three were conferred before the issue was quashed. It is probably the rarest gallantry award.

Sir Henry Evelyn Wood (1838–1919), bedecked with honours and awards after a lifetime of service. Famously rising 'from Midshipman to Field Marshal', he began his career in the Royal Navy. After being severely wounded before Sebastopol in 1855 he transferred into the cavalry and won his Victoria Cross at Sindhora in India on 29th December 1859.

with Nursing and Hospital Services ('in the presence of the enemy') and to civilians serving with the Forces.

Royal Warrant of 5th February 1931 approved the wearing of a half-sized miniature Victoria Cross when miniatures were worn. The possible forfeiture and restoration of the award was to be discretionary.

Royal Warrant of 9th May 1938 made provision for the award of the Victoria Cross to the Burma Military Forces following Burma's separation from India for administrative purposes.

Royal Warrant of 24th January 1941 extended the award to the new Indian Air Force.

Air combat was pioneered in the warfare of 1914–18 and there were nineteen awards of the Victoria Cross for air combat. In this scene Captain Lanoe Hawker DSO (1890–1916), Royal Flying Corps, is shown in the Victoria Cross action on 25th July 1915, when he attacked three German aeroplanes in succession, bringing down two of them. Hawker fell victim to Germany's leading air ace Manfred von Richthofen in 1916.

The VC group of Sergeant Alfred J. Richards (1880–1953): one of the famous six awards to the Lancashire Fusiliers chosen by ballot for the 'Lancashire Landings' on Gallipoli, 25th April 1915 (see page 52). Richards had fought his way ashore under terrifically heavy fire and when severely wounded. He has three medals for the First World War, the 1939–45 Defence Medal, the 1937 Coronation Medal and the Army Long Service and Good Conduct Medal. Discharged because of his wounds in 1915, he had served for twenty years.

Royal Warrant of 31st December 1942 extended the award to the Home Guard and similar forces, as well as to paramilitary forces in India and Burma (for example frontier constabularies and militias) and to Women's Auxiliary Services.

Royal Warrant of 30th September 1961 reflected changes within the Empire and Commonwealth and allowed that service personnel of Commonwealth countries were eligible for the Victoria Cross. Changes to the gratuity were also announced.

Royal Warrant of 24th March 1964 transferred the functions of the Secretary of State for War relating to the Victoria Cross to the Secretary of State for Defence.

The miniature medal group of Lieutenant Alexis Doxat (1867–1942), 3rd Imperial Yeomanry: Victoria Cross, Queen's South Africa Medal, three medals for 1914–18 and 1937 Coronation. He won his Victoria Cross in the action at Zeerust on 20th October 1900 during the Boer War, when he rescued under heavy fire a trooper who had fallen from his horse.

The Victoria Cross by campaign

Since its inception in 1856, 1355 awards of the Victoria Cross have been made – 833 to the Army, 107 to the Royal Navy, fifty-one to the Royal Air Force and other air forces, ten to the Royal Marines, four to civilians and the remainder to Imperial and Commonwealth forces. Of these, 522 awards were made before 1914, including 348 to the British Army, forty-three to British Naval and Marine forces, ninety-five to East India Company or Indian Army units, thirty-two to Dominion and Colonial troops and four to civilians.

The table below gives a breakdown of Victoria Crosses awarded by campaign.

The Russian War (Baltic, Azoff and Crimea), 1854–6	111
Middle East: the Persian campaign, 1856–7	3
India: the Indian Mutiny, 1857–9	182
New Zealand: the Maori Wars, 1860–6	15
China War, 1860	7
China: the Tai Ping rebellion, 1862	1
North West Frontier of India: Umbeyla, 1863	2
Japan (Shimonoseki), 1864	3
North East Frontier of India: the Bhutan Campaign, 1864–5	2
Canada, 1866 (ammunition fire)	1
West Africa: Gambia, 1866	1
Indian Ocean: Andaman Islands, 1867	5
North East Africa: the Abyssinian Campaign, 1867–8	2

A rescue under fire during the Maori Wars in New Zealand. During the attack on the Maori stockade or 'pah' at Te Papa, Tauranga, on 29th April 1864, Samuel Mitchell (1841–94), Captain of the Foretop of HMS Harrier, carried Commander Hay, mortally wounded, out of the action. This was done under heavy and close fire and after Mitchell had been ordered by Hay to leave him and seek shelter.

North East Frontier of India:	
Looshai operations, 1872	1
West Africa: the Ashantee War, 1873–4	4
Malaya: Perak operations, 1874–5	1
North West Frontier of India:	
Baluchistan, 1877	1
South Africa: the Cape Frontier Wars, 1877–8	1
Afghanistan: the Second Afghan War, 1878–80	16
South Africa: the Zulu War, 1879	23
North East Frontier of India: Naga, 1879–80	1
South Africa: the Basuto Campaign, 1879–81	6
South Africa: Transvaal War (First Boer War), 1880–1	6
North Africa: the Invasion of Egypt, 1882	3

The Victoria Cross group of Lieutenant (later Major General) A. T. Moore, 3rd Bombay Light Cavalry (1830–1913). He won his VC for his bravery in attacking a 'square' of infantry at the battle of Khushab in Persia in February 1857. Also shown are his Order of the Bath (CB), India General Service Medal with clasp for Persia 1857, medal for the Indian Mutiny with clasp 'Central India' and the 1902 Coronation medal.

The Victoria Cross group of Captain John Cook, 5th Gurkhas (1843–79). He was awarded the Cross during the initial phase of the Second Afghan War when in the assault on the Peiwar Kotal, 2nd December 1878, he saved the life of another officer by engaging in hand-to-hand combat with his assailants. Cook was killed on 13th December 1879 near Kabul. Shown here are his India General Service medal (1854–95), with clasps Umbeyla and North West Frontier for earlier Indian frontier warfare, and his Afghan medal with three clasps.

North East Africa: operations in the Sudan, 1884–5	5
Burma: frontier tribal operations, 1888–9	2
North West Frontier of India: Hunza, 1891	3
North East Frontier of India: Manipur, 1891	1
West Africa: Gambia River operations, 1892	1
Burma: Kachin Hills operations, 1892–3	1
North West Frontier of India: Chitral, 1895	1
Southern Africa: Matabeleland and Mashonaland, 1895–6	3
North East Africa: the reconquest of the Sudan, 1896–8	5
North West Frontier of India: tribal uprisings of 1897–8	11
Mediterranean: the occupation of Crete, 1898	1
South Africa: the Second Boer War, 1899–1902	78
West Africa: the Third Ashanti War, 1900	2
China: the Boxer Rebellion, 1900	2
North East Africa: Somaliland operations, 1902–4	6
West Africa: operations in Northern Nigeria, 1903	1
The Tibet Expedition, 1903–4	1
First World War, 1914–18	628
Russian Civil War: intervention in northern Russia, 1919	5
Middle East: the Iraq Revolt, 1919–20	1
North West Frontier of India: Waziristan operations, 1919–21	3

Lance Corporal William Gordon (1864–1922), West India Regiment, wins the Victoria Cross by saving the life of Major Madden. During the attack on Toniataba, Gambia River, West Africa, on 13th March 1892, Gordon placed himself between his officer and a volley of enemy rifles, receiving a severe chest wound. From its inception the Victoria Cross was not confined to European troops but did exclude Indian soldiers, who were deemed to have their own gallantry award in the form of the Order of Merit (see page 8). They were not admitted to the Victoria Cross until 1911.

Right: *Lance Corporal Michael O'Leary (1890–1961) wins the Irish Guards' first Victoria Cross, at Cuinchy on 1st February 1915. In an astonishing display of personal gallantry in attacking German defence lines, he 'practically captured the enemy's position by himself', killed or captured ten Germans and 'prevented the rest of the attacking party from being fired upon'.*

Private William Young (1876–1916), 8th East Lancashire Regiment. Although suffering terrible wounds to his face and chest, Young persevered in his attempt to rescue a wounded man under very heavy fire near Fouquevillers on 22nd December 1915. Many Victoria Crosses for the Western Front were awarded for this sort of selfless action in rescuing men under fire.

The magnificent medal group of Subadar Major Ishar Singh (1895–1963). As a Sepoy (Private) in the 28th Punjabis he won the Victoria Cross for gallantry on 10th April 1921 at Haidari Kach during the Indian frontier campaign in Waziristan. He not only recovered and kept in action his Lewis gun while severely wounded, but tended and fetched water for other casualties under fire, refusing to be evacuated. He has medals for 1914–18, for the North West Frontier and for the Second World War.

North West Frontier of India: the Mohmand campaign, 1935	1
Second World War, 1939–45	182
The Korean War, 1951–3	4
The Vietnam War, 1959–72	4
Malaysia: anti-terrorist operations, 1963–6	1
The South Atlantic (Falklands) campaign, 1982	2
Occupation of Iraq, 2004	1
(United States, Unknown Warrior)	1

Sergeant Harold Whitfield (1886–1956) of the Shropshire Yeomanry and 10th King's Shropshire Light Infantry, wearing dress miniatures. These are worn on formal occasions in place of the heavier originals. His Victoria Cross was awarded for gallantry at Burj-el-Lisaneh, Palestine, in March 1918, when he single-handedly captured a Turkish machine-gun position.

Examples of citations

It is impossible to generalise about the nature of the incidents for which the Victoria Cross was awarded – the circumstances naturally vary from action to action. The following selection, covering the entire history of the Victoria Cross, gives just a glimpse of the levels of extraordinary gallantry that have been required to earn 'the Bronze Cross'.

The Crimean War, 1854–6

The first Victoria Cross awards were made for the campaign against Russia, 1854–6. In total 111 were awarded.

SERGEANT MAJOR ANDREW HENRY, ROYAL ARTILLERY

At the Battle of Inkermann [5th November 1854], he defended the guns of his battery against overwhelming numbers of the enemy who attacked his position at the point of the bayonet. He wrestled a bayonet from one of the Russians, threw the man down and fought against the other assailants before he was stabbed in his chest, arms and back. He received twelve bayonet wounds. He was at the time Sergeant Major of 'G' Battery, 2nd Division.

(*The London Gazette*, 24th February 1857)

The unique group of Able Seaman Joseph Trewavas (1835–1905), Royal Navy. He was awarded the Conspicuous Gallantry Medal (to the right of the Victoria Cross) for gallantry in the Azoff Campaign in 1855 and, on the creation of the Victoria Cross, also received the new Cross for the same incident. This is the only example of such a double award for one action; it was usual to cancel the earlier award of a 'lesser' decoration if the action was subsequently elevated to Victoria Cross status. He also received the French Legion of Honour (second from right). The group sold for £29,000 in London in 1996.

Lieutenant Fred Roberts (later Field Marshal Lord Roberts), Bengal Horse Artillery, wins his Victoria Cross at Khodagunge on 2nd January 1858 during the Indian Mutiny. He attacked a party of mutineers and cut them down, capturing their standard. Roberts's letters make it clear how determined he was to win one of the new awards. A driving ambition to possess the Victoria Cross is frequently encountered in officers' correspondence and was something the War Office tried to discourage, as it seemed likely to lead to reckless behaviour.

PLAYER'S CIGARETTES

LIEUT. F. S. ROBERTS AT KHODAGUNGE. 1858.

The Indian Mutiny, 1857–9

The army historian Sir John Fortescue said that the Victoria Cross 'came of age' during the Indian Mutiny, and no fewer than 182 were awarded for the campaign of 1857–9. This large number reflects both the ferocity of the fighting on occasion and the significance attached to the campaign as a whole.

LIEUTENANT J. A. TYTLER, 66TH (GOORKHA) REGIMENT, BENGAL NATIVE INFANTRY

On the attacking parties approaching the enemy's position under a heavy fire of round shot, grape and musketry, on the occasion of the action at Choopoorah on 10th February last [1858], Lt. Tytler dashed on horseback ahead of all and alone, up to the enemy's guns, where he remained engaged hand-to-hand, until they were carried by us, and where he was shot through the left arm, had a spear wound in his chest and a ball through the right sleeve of his coat.

(*The London Gazette*, 24th August 1858)

The Zulu War, 1879

The brief campaign against the Zulu, January–July 1879, resulted in the award of twenty-three Victoria Crosses. The operations included perhaps the most famous Victoria Cross action of all time, the defence of the mission station at Rorke's Drift, 22nd–23rd January 1879, for which no fewer than eleven Crosses were conferred. This is the largest number awarded for a single action.

Lord William de la Poer Beresford in single combat with a Zulu. Captain Lord Beresford (1847–1900), 9th Lancers, was awarded the Victoria Cross for this action on the Umvolosi River on 3rd July 1879, when he and Sergeant E. O'Toole, Frontier Light Horse, who also received the VC, rescued a wounded trooper who had fallen from his horse and fought their way to safety. Beresford was on leave from the Afghan War at the time!

CORPORAL F. C. SCHIESS, NATAL NATIVE CONTINGENT

For conspicuous gallantry in the defence of Rorke's Drift Post on the night of 22nd January 1879 when, in spite of his having been wounded in the foot a few days previously, he greatly distinguished himself when the garrison were repulsing, with the bayonet, a series of desperate assaults made by the Zulus, and displayed great activity and devoted gallantry throughout the defence. On one occasion, when the garrison had retired to the inner line of defence and the Zulus occupied the wall of mealie bags which had been abandoned, he crept along the wall, without any order, to dislodge a Zulu who was shooting better than usual and succeeded in killing him and two others before he, the Corporal, returned to the inner defence.

(*The London Gazette*, 29th November 1879)

Schiess was the first foreigner to win the Victoria Cross and the first member of a South African unit to receive the award. His medal is displayed in the National Army Museum, Chelsea.

The South African (Second Boer) War, 1899–1902

This, the largest of Britain's Imperial campaigns, involved the first large-scale deployment of contingents from Canada, Australia, New Zealand and other colonies. A large number of the seventy-eight Victoria Crosses awarded during the South African War were for rescuing wounded men under fire.

Two prominent British generals of the Boer War, celebrated as 'Heroes of Our Time' on contemporary cigarette cards. On the left is General Sir George White (awarded his Victoria Cross for the Battle of Charasiah, Second Afghan War, 6th October 1879), famous as the defender of Ladysmith during the Boer War. On the right is Lord Roberts, then Commander-in-Chief in South Africa, who won his VC in 1858 (see page 27).

'Saving the guns at Colenso', 15th December 1899. One of the severe British reverses during 'Black Week' in the Second Boer War. Seven Victoria Crosses were awarded for this attempt to recover under heavy fire the guns of the 7th, 14th and 66th Batteries, Royal Field Artillery.

CORPORAL JOHN J. CLEMENTS, RIMINGTON'S GUIDES

On the 24th February 1901, near Strijdenburg, when dangerously wounded through the lungs and called upon to surrender, Corpl. Clements threw himself into the midst of a party of five Boers, shooting three of them with his revolver and thereby causing the whole party to surrender to himself and two unwounded men of Rimington's Guides.

(*The London Gazette*, 4th June 1901)

CORPORAL HENRY J. KNIGHT, 1ST LIVERPOOL REGIMENT

On 21st August 1900, during operations near Van Wyk's Vlei, Corpl. Knight was posted to some rocks with four men covering the right rear of a detachment of the same company who, under Capt. Ewart, were holding the right of the line. The enemy, about 50 strong, attacked Capt. Ewart's right and almost surrounded, at short range, Corpl. Knight's small party. That NCO held his ground, directing his party to retire one by one to better cover, where he maintained his position for nearly an hour, covering the withdrawal of Capt. Ewart's force, and losing two of his four men. He then retired, bringing with him two wounded men. One of these he left in a place of safety, the other he carried for nearly two miles. The party was hotly engaged during the whole time.

(*The London Gazette*, 4th January 1901)

The First World War, 1914–18

During the 'Great War' 628 Victoria Crosses were awarded to British and Imperial forces – the largest number for any single conflict, though this is hardly surprising given the nature and extent of the war. The first was conferred upon Lieutenant Maurice Dease, 4th Royal Fusiliers, for an action on 23rd August 1914 and was one of five awarded for that day. The last was given to Major B. Cloutman, Royal Engineers, for an action at Pont-sur-Sambre, France, on 6th November 1918. We should bear in mind that some posthumous awards were made after the end of the war, an example being that to Lieutenant W. Macrae Bruce, 59th Rifles,

Intensely patriotic war magazines and part-works, such as 'The War Illustrated' or the one shown here, 'Deeds that Thrill the Empire', glorified the actions of Britain's forces during the 1914–18 war and perpetuated stories of gallantry and heroism.

The Victoria Cross and medal group of Private F. G. Miles (1896–1961), Gloucestershire Regiment. Miles was awarded the VC for single-handledly attacking and destroying German machine-gun posts near Bois L'Eveque on 23rd October 1918. His actions allowed his Company to advance and resulted in the capture of sixteen machine guns and fifty-nine Germans.

Private Sidney Godley, 4th Royal Fusiliers, was another early Great War winner of the Victoria Cross – for gallantry in keeping his machine-gun in action for two hours, although wounded, at Mons on 23rd August 1914. He is believed by some to have been the model for Bruce Bairnsfather's famous cartoon character 'Old Bill'.

Indian Army, who was awarded the Victoria Cross in September 1919 for an action in December 1914 in which he had been killed.

Most (503) of the Great War Victoria Crosses were granted for the familiar trench warfare of the Western Front, in Flanders and France, but the international roll-call of awards reflects the fact that this was a world war: there were twenty-three for Mesopotamia (Iraq), eighteen for Gallipoli, fourteen for Egypt and Palestine, four for East Africa, four for Italy, two for Salonika, two for operations on the North West Frontier of India and one for West Africa.

Nineteen awards were made for air combat and forty-two for naval actions, the latter including major sea battles such as Jutland, operations at Zeebrugge and Ostend and in support of land campaigns in East Africa, Iraq and Gallipoli.

Apart from the usual land and sea operations, new and terrible ways of waging war were practised during the First World War – for example the use of poison gas and flame-throwers, the employment of submarines and fighting aircraft and the introduction of the tank. Many of these new developments in warfare were reflected in awards of the Victoria Cross.

Infantry preparing for an attack on the Western Front. Over five hundred Victoria Crosses (out of the 628 awarded for 1914–18) were given for gallantry in the 'France and Flanders theatre' on the Western Front.

While a world war raged elsewhere it was business as usual on the North West Frontier of India, where tribal disturbances and operations continued. In this incident – prompting one of two Victoria Crosses for the Frontier – Private Charles Hull (1890–1953) of the 21st Lancers rescues an officer under the close fire of the enemy after a cavalry charge at Hafiz Khor. The other Frontier Victoria Cross was a posthumous award made to Captain E. Jotham (1883–1915), 51st Sikhs, for gallantry at Spin Khaisora in the Tochi Valley on 7th January 1915.

An early First World War Victoria Cross: blowing the bridge at Jemappes, 23rd August 1914. During the initial German offensive and the British 'retreat to Mons', bridges were destroyed to impede the German advance. At Jemappes, Lance Corporal Alfred Jarvis (1881–1948), Royal Engineers, worked under close enemy fire for an hour and a half and fired the demolition charges that destroyed the bridge.

The medals of Petty Officer Ernest Pitcher (1888–1946), Royal Naval Reserve, which include the Victoria Cross, the Distinguished Service Medal, the French Medaille Militaire and the French Croix-de-Guerre. Pitcher was awarded the Victoria Cross by ballot (see page 60) for his part in the 'Q' Ship action by HMS Dunraven on 8th August 1917. 'Q' Ships – or 'mystery ships' – were another new feature of 1914–18. They were ostensibly unarmed merchantmen, intended to lure enemy submarines to the surface as easy victims, at which point they would reveal their hidden guns and destroy the submarine. Pitcher was part of the ship's gun crew that engaged an enemy U-boat in the Bay of Biscay.

LIEUTENANT A. B. SMITH, ROYAL NAVAL RESERVE

For most conspicuous gallantry and devotion to duty when in command of the S.S. *Otaki* on 10th March 1917. At about 2.30 p.m., the S.S. *Otaki*, whose armament consisted of one 4.7" gun for defensive purposes, sighted the German raider *Moewe*, which was armed with four 5.9", one 4.1" and two 22-pounder guns and two torpedo tubes. The *Moewe* kept the *Otaki* under observation for some time and finally called upon her to stop. This Lieut. Smith refused to do and a duel ensued at ranges of 1900–2000 yards and lasted for about twenty minutes. During this action, the *Otaki* scored several hits on the *Moewe*, causing considerable damage and starting a fire, which lasted for three days. *Otaki* sustained several casualties and received much damage herself and was heavily on fire. Lt. Smith therefore gave orders for the boats to be lowered to allow the crew to be rescued. He remained on board the ship himself and went down with her when she sank with the British colours still flying, after what was described in an enemy account as 'a duel as gallant as naval history can relate'.

(*The London Gazette*, 24th May 1919)

CAPTAIN E. N. F. BELL, 9TH ROYAL INNISKILLING FUSILIERS AND 109 TRENCH MORTAR BATTERY

For most conspicuous bravery. He was in command of a trench mortar battery and advanced with the infantry in the attack. When our front line was held up by enfilading machine gun fire, Capt. Bell crept forward and shot the machine gunner. Later, on no less than three occasions, when our

Like air combat and the use of tanks, poison gas and flame-throwers, undersea warfare was new to the First World War. In this scene the submarine E-14, under Lieutenant Commander E. C. Boyle (1883–1967), operates in the Sea of Marmora against Turkish shipping. The danger from Turkish naval patrols and, as here, from underwater minefields was very great but the submarine succeeded in sinking three enemy vessels. Four Victoria Crosses were awarded for submarine actions during the war, two of them to E-14 – one to Boyle for this operation and one granted posthumously to Lieutenant Commander G. S. White (1886–1918) for an incident in 1918.

bombing parties which were clearing the enemy's trenches were unable to advance, he went forward alone and threw trench-mortar bombs among the enemy. When he had no more bombs available, he stood on the parapet under intense fire and used a rifle with great coolness and effect on the enemy advancing to counter-attack. Finally he was killed rallying and reorganising infantry parties which had lost their officers. All this was outside the scope of his normal duties with his battery. He gave his life in his supreme devotion to duty.

(*The London Gazette*, 29th September 1916)

Captain Bell received one of nine Victoria Crosses awarded for the fighting on the infamous First Day of the Battle of the Somme, 1st July 1916. Six of the nine were posthumous.

'L' Battery, Royal Horse Artillery, in their famous stand at Nery on 1st September 1914. Three Victoria Crosses were awarded to men of the battery for their gallantry in keeping the guns in action in the face of overwhelming odds until their ammunition was expended and most of the gun crews were killed or wounded. The various branches of the Royal Regiment of Artillery – the Royal Horse Artillery, Royal Field Artillery and Royal Garrison Artillery – played a major role in the fighting in France and Flanders as well as in other battlefields and won twenty Victoria Crosses during the war.

'The new Leviathan': tanks in action on the Western Front. These awesome weapons were first unleashed at Flers in September 1916 and initially had the desired effect of scattering terrified enemy forces. Two Victoria Crosses were awarded to the Tank Corps – to Captain R. Wain (1896–1917) and Captain C. Robertson (1890–1917). Both were posthumous.

ACTING CAPTAIN R. W. L. WAIN, TANK CORPS

For most conspicuous bravery in command of a section of Tanks. During an attack, his Tank was disabled by a direct hit near an enemy strong point which was holding up the attack. Capt. Wain and one man, both seriously wounded, were the only survivors. Though bleeding profusely from his wounds, he refused the attention of stretcher-bearers, rushed from behind the Tank with a Lewis gun and captured the strong point, taking about half the garrison prisoners. Although his wounds were very serious, he picked up a rifle and continued to fire at the retiring enemy until he received a fatal wound in the head. It was due to the valour displayed by Capt. Wain that the infantry were able to advance.

(*The London Gazette*, 13th February 1918)

ACTING CAPTAIN F. M. F. WEST, MC, ROYAL MUNSTER FUSILIERS AND ROYAL FLYING CORPS

In recognition of his outstanding bravery in aerial combat. Capt. West, while engaging hostile aircraft at a low altitude far over the enemy's lines, was attacked by seven aircraft. Early in the engagement, one of his legs was partially severed by an explosive bullet and fell powerless into the controls, rendering the machine for the time unmanageable. Lifting his disabled leg, he regained control of the machine and although wounded in the other leg he, with surpassing bravery and devotion to duty, manoeuvred his machine so skilfully that his observer was

Flight Sub-Lieutenant Reginald Warneford (1891–1915) of the Royal Naval Air Service was awarded the Victoria Cross for his single-handed destruction of a Zeppelin airship, which he had pursued from the Belgian coast to Ghent, on 7th June 1915. He dropped bombs on the airship from a height of only 200 feet (61 metres) and damaged his own aeroplane in the process. Warneford was killed in an air accident only ten days later.

Stories and images of the nation's Victoria Cross heroes were regularly put before the public in patriotic contemporary magazines such as 'The Great War', one of many popular part-works brought out to exploit the demand for information about the war.

enabled to get several good bursts into the enemy machines, which drove them away. Capt. West then, with rare courage and determination, desperately wounded as he was, brought his machine over our lines and landed safely. Exhausted by his exertions, he fainted, but on regaining consciousness, insisted on writing his report.

(*The London Gazette*, 8th November 1918)

This was one of nineteen Victoria Crosses awarded for air combat. The Royal Flying Corps amalgamated with the Royal Naval Air Service to form the Royal Air Force on 1st April 1918.

SEPOY (LATER SUBADAR MAJOR) KHUDADAD KHAN, 129TH BALUCHIS, INDIAN ARMY

On 31st October 1914 at Hollebeke, Belgium, the British Officer in charge of the detachment having been wounded, and the other gun put out of action by a shell, Sepoy Khudadad, although himself wounded, remained working his gun until all the other five men of gun detachment had been killed.

(*The London Gazette*, 7th December 1914)

This was the first Victoria Cross conferred upon an Indian soldier, following the extension of the award to Indians in 1911. Khudadad Khan, who was left for dead by the Germans, was awarded the Cross while all the other men of his detachment received posthumous decorations for gallantry. There were eleven awards of the Victoria Cross to Indians in the First World War.

The incident in which Khudadad Khan won the Victoria Cross, illustrated in a contemporary magazine.

Australian soldiers on the Somme in 1916. Imperial contingents from all over the world – India, Australia, Canada, New Zealand, the West Indies, Ceylon and Africa – played a leading role in the fighting in all of the many theatres of the First World War.

LANCE-CORPORAL ALBERT JACKA, 1ST BATTALION, AUSTRALIAN IMPERIAL FORCE

For most conspicuous bravery on the night of 19th–20th May 1915, at Courtney's Post, Gallipoli Peninsula. L. Cpl. Jacka, while holding a portion of a trench with four other men, was heavily attacked. When all except himself were killed or wounded, the trench was rushed and occupied by seven Turks. L. Cpl. Jacka at once most gallantly attacked them single-handed and killed the whole party, five by rifle fire and two with the bayonet.

(The London Gazette, 24th July 1915)

Lance-Corporal Jacka's Victoria Cross was one of eighteen awarded for the fighting at Gallipoli in 1915, in which Australian troops were heavily engaged. Australian troops were awarded no fewer than sixty-two Victoria Crosses for service at Gallipoli or on the Western Front.

Inter-war awards, 1919–39

Between the world wars British and Indian armies undertook active service in the Russian Civil War, 1919–20 (five Victoria Crosses awarded), in Iraq and Kurdistan, 1919–20 (one Victoria

In the initial attacks on the first day of the Battle of Loos, 25th September 1915, Piper D. Laidlaw's battalion, the 7th King's Own Scottish Borderers, was confronted by poison gas and heavy artillery fire. Laidlaw led the assault from the trenches, playing the Regimental March and Charge. Although badly wounded in both legs, he followed his comrades towards their objective until the severity of his wounds forced him to withdraw. He was subsequently honoured as 'The Piper of Loos' and awarded a Victoria Cross.

The Victoria Cross group of Lieutenant W. D. Kenny (1899–1920), 4–39th Garwhal Rifles. Kenny was awarded a posthumous Victoria Cross for his gallantry in defence of an outpost in Waziristan, North West Frontier of India, on 20th January 1920. The post came under repeated heavy attacks and there was fierce hand-to-hand fighting. Kenny was killed leading a counter-attack as his party withdrew. His medals are shown mounted for wear in the order as worn by his mother.

Cross for Iraq), on the North West Frontier of India, 1919–21 and 1935 (four Victoria Crosses), and in Palestine, 1936-9.

CAPTAIN GODFREY MEYNELL, 5TH BATTALION, 12TH FRONTIER FORCE REGIMENT, INDIAN ARMY

For most conspicuous gallantry and extreme devotion to duty. On the 29th Sept. 1935, while operating against Mohmand tribesmen in the attack on Point 4080, Capt. Meynell was Adjutant of the Battalion. In the final phase of the attack, the Battalion Commander was unable to get information from his most forward troops. Capt. Meynell went forward to ascertain the situation and found the forward troops on the objective but involved in a struggle against an enemy vastly superior in numbers. Seeing the situation, he at once took command of the men in this area. The enemy by this time was closing in on the position from three sides. Capt. Meynell had at his disposal two Lewis guns and about 30 men. Although this party was maintaining heavy and accurate fire on the advancing enemy, the overwhelming numbers of the latter succeeded in reaching the position. Both Lewis guns were damaged beyond repair and a fierce hand-to-hand struggle commenced. During the struggle, Capt. Meynell was mortally wounded and all his men were either killed or wounded.

Throughout the action, Capt. Meynell endeavoured by all means to communicate the situation to HQ but determined to hold on at all costs and encouraged his men to fight with him to the last. By so doing he inflicted on the enemy very heavy casualties which prevented them from exploiting their success. The fine example Capt. Meynell set to his men, coupled with his determination to hold the position to the last, maintain the traditions of the Army and reflect the highest credit on the fallen officer and his comrades.

(*The London Gazette*, 24th December 1935)

Meynell had already won the Military Cross in action on the North West Frontier in 1933. His posthumous Victoria Cross was presented to his mother by the uncrowned King Edward VIII – the only Victoria Cross of his reign.

The Second World War, 1939–45

During the Second World War 182 Victoria Crosses were awarded to British and Imperial forces. This is far fewer than in the First World War, reflecting not only the fact that a different type of warfare was being waged but also that there was a greater range of gallantry awards available for issue – and that the Victoria Cross was becoming increasingly difficult to earn.

These awards include the following: seven for France and Belgium, 1939–40; three for Norway, 1940; four for Somaliland and Abyssinia, 1941; five for Greece and Crete, 1941; two for Syria (Vichy French territory), 1941; one for Hong Kong, 1941; two for Malaya before the fall of Singapore in 1942; five for the commando raid on St Nazaire, 1942; sixteen for North Africa, 1941–3; thirteen for operations in Tunisia in 1942–3; three for the Dieppe Raid, 1942; seven to Australians for New Guinea, 1942–5; twenty-seven for Burma, 1942–5; twenty for Italy, 1943–5; sixteen for north-west Europe, 1944–5; three for the Solomon Islands, 1944–5; five for Arnhem, 1944; two for Borneo, 1945.

The thirty-two Victoria Crosses awarded to aerial forces reflect the prominent part played by the Royal Air Force and Commonwealth air forces in a variety of roles including home defence, coastal command, supporting land operations and in the strategic bombing of Germany's industrial centres. The Royal Navy

The first gazetted Victoria Cross of the Second World War: Captain B. A. W. Warburton-Lee, Royal Navy (1895–1940). Commanding HMS Hardy, he led five destroyers into a Norwegian fjord near Narvik during a blinding blizzard on 10th April 1940. Here he made three attacks on warships and merchantmen and finally engaged five larger German warships. He was killed during the action.

Naik YESHWANT GHADGE, V.C. (Posthumous),
5th Mahratta Light Infantry.

Naik Yeshwant Ghadge (1921–44), 3–5th Mahratta Light Infantry, received a posthumous Victoria Cross for his gallantry in the upper Tiber Valley on 10th July 1944 when, although seriously wounded, he single-handedly attacked and destroyed a German machine-gun position. He died of his wounds.

The VC group of Warrant Officer N. C. Jackson (1919–94) of 106 Squadron, RAF. Returning from a raid on Schweinfurt on the night of 26th–27th April 1944, Jackson's Lancaster was attacked by a night fighter and a wing petrol tank caught fire. At 20,000 feet, Jackson, although wounded, climbed out along the fuselage and on to the wing to try to put out the fire. As the fire spread, Jackson was severely burned and eventually blown off the wing. He was last seen falling to the ground with his parachute in flames. Remarkably, he survived the descent, though severely injured, and became a prisoner of war.

was equally engaged in vital operations, for example the destruction of surface raiders such as the *Bismarck* and the *Tirpitz*, providing air support to the convoy system and supporting land operations across the globe. Naval personnel won twenty-two Victoria Crosses during the war.

ACTING FLIGHT LIEUTENANT RODERICK ALASTAIR BROOK LEAROYD, 49 SQUADRON, ROYAL AIR FORCE

In recognition of most conspicuous bravery. This officer, as first pilot of a Hampden aircraft, has repeatedly shown the highest conception of his duty and complete indifference to personal danger in making attacks at the

Two Burma Victoria Crosses. Naik (Corporal) Gian Singh, 15th Punjabis (left), won his on the Kamye-Myingyan road, Burma, on 2nd March 1945, when he single-handedly attacked a series of Japanese positions though wounded. Rifleman Bhanbhagta Gurung, 2nd Gurkhas (right), won his on 5th March 1945 at 'Snowdon East' when he personally destroyed five enemy foxholes and machine-gun posts and then beat off a Japanese counter-attack. His actions were decisive in the capture of the objective.

Left: *Five Victoria Cross winners of the Second World War after their award ceremony at Buckingham Palace in June 1945. They are (left to right): Lieutenant B. C. G. Place, VC, DSC, Royal Navy (submarine attack on the Tirpitz, 22nd September 1943); Lieutenant Commander S. H. Beattie, Royal Navy (HMS Campbeltown, St Nazaire raid, 27th–28th March 1942); Lance Corporal H. Nicholls (Belgium, 21st May 1940); Lieutenant D. Cameron, Royal Navy Reserve (submarine attack on the Tirpitz, 22nd September 1943) and (seated) Major F. A. Tilston, Canadian Infantry (Hochwald Forest, Germany, 1st March 1945).*

Right and below: *Two depictions of Private James Stokes (1915–45), 2nd King's Shropshire Light Infantry, who received a posthumous Victoria Cross after leading successive attacks on fortified German positions until mortally wounded in an attack on German positions near Kervenheim on 1st March 1945. Below, a painting by Terence Cuneo shows the final stage of his actions. On the right, a popular children's comic retells the story of Private Stokes, who had become something of a folk hero. Victoria Cross winners are understandably honoured and celebrated within the community at local and national levels and the memory of their exploits can be perpetuated in many ways, formal and informal.*

lowest altitudes regardless of opposition. On the night of the 12th August 1940, he was detailed to attack a special objective on the Dortmund-Ems canal. He had attacked this objective on a previous occasion and was well aware of the risks entailed. To achieve success it was necessary to approach from a direction well known to the enemy, through a lane of especially disposed anti-aircraft defences and in the face of the most intense point-blank fire from guns of all calibres. The reception of the previous aircraft might well have deterred the stoutest heart, all being hit and two lost. Flt. Lt. Learoyd nevertheless made his attack at 150 feet, his aircraft being repeatedly hit and large pieces of the main plane torn away. He was almost blinded by the glare of many searchlights at close range but pressed home his attack with the greatest resolution and skill. He subsequently brought his wrecked aircraft home and as the landing flaps were inoperative and the undercarriage indicators out of action, waited for dawn in the vicinity of his aerodrome before landing, which he accomplished without causing injury to his crew or further damage to the aircraft. The high courage, skill and determination which this officer has invariably displayed on many occasions in the face of the enemy sets an example which is unsurpassed.

(The London Gazette, 20th August 1940)

The Victoria Cross, Distinguished Flying Cross group awarded to Flying Officer L. A. Trigg (1914–43), Royal New Zealand Air Force. Trigg, flying a Liberator of 200 Squadron, Coastal Command, won a posthumous Victoria Cross for his gallantry in persisting with an attack against the German submarine U-468 off West Africa on 27th October 1943 even though his aircraft was already in flames.

This was one of thirty-one Victoria Crosses awarded to Bomber Command during the war. Of thirty-two air Victoria Crosses for 1939–45, twenty-two went to the Royal Air Force, the others to Commonwealth air forces. Remarkably, only one Victoria Cross was awarded to Fighter Command – that to Flight Lieutenant E. J. B. Nicolson, 249 Squadron, for gallantry over Southampton on 16th August 1940. His was also the only 'Battle of Britain' Victoria Cross.

FLYING OFFICER LLOYD ALLAN TRIGG, ROYAL NEW ZEALAND AIR FORCE

Flying Officer Trigg has rendered outstanding service on Convoy, Escort and Anti-Submarine Duties. He has completed 46 operational sorties and has invariably displayed skill and courage of a high order. One day in Aug. 1943, FO Trigg as Captain and Pilot, flew a patrol in a Liberator bomber,

although he had not previously made any operational sorties in that type of aircraft. After searching for eight hours the Liberator sighted a surfaced U-Boat. FO Trigg immediately prepared to attack. During the approach the aircraft received many hits from the submarine's anti-aircraft guns and burst into flames, which quickly enveloped the tail. The moment was critical. FO Trigg could have broken off the engagement and made a forced landing in the sea, but if he continued the attack the aircraft would present a no-deflection target to deadly anti-aircraft fire and every second spent in the air would increase the extent and intensity of the flames and diminish the chances of survival. There could have been no hesitation or doubt in his mind. He maintained his course in spite of the already precarious condition of his aircraft and executed a masterly attack. Skimming over the U-Boat at less than 50 feet, with anti-aircraft fire entering his open bomb doors, FO Trigg dropped his bombs on and around the U-Boat, where they exploded with devastating effect. A short distance further on, the Liberator dived into the sea with her gallant Captain and crew. The U-Boat sank within twenty minutes and some of her crew were picked up later in a rubber dinghy that had broken loose from the Liberator. The Battle of the Atlantic has yielded many fine stories of air attacks on underwater craft, but FO Trigg's exploit stands out as an epic of grim determination and high courage. His was the path of duty that leads to glory.

(The London Gazette, 2nd November 1943)

This Victoria Cross is unique in that the circumstances, and thus the award recommendation that followed, were reported by the enemy – German survivors of the attacked U-boat.

TEMPORARY CAPTAIN JOHN NEIL RANDLE, NORFOLK REGIMENT

On 4th May 1944 at Kohima, in Assam, a Battalion of the Norfolk Regiment attacked the Japanese positions on a nearby ridge. Capt. Randle took over the command of the Company which was leading the attack when the Company Commander was severely wounded. His handling of a difficult situation in the face of heavy fire was masterly and although wounded himself in the knee by grenade splinters he continued to inspire his men by his initiative, courage and outstanding leadership until the Company had captured its objective and consolidated its position. He then went forward and brought in all the wounded men who were lying outside the perimeter.

In spite of his painful wound, Capt. Randle refused to be evacuated and insisted on carrying out a personal reconnaissance

Burma 1944: the severe campaign to expel the Japanese after their startling advance towards India in 1942–3 led to the award of twenty-seven Victoria Crosses for Burma to British and Imperial forces.

with great daring in bright moonlight prior to a further attack by his Company on the positions to which the enemy had withdrawn.

At dawn on 6th May the attack opened, led by Capt. Randle, and one of the platoons succeeded in reaching the crest of the hill held by the Japanese. Another platoon, however, ran into heavy medium machine gun fire from a bunker on the reverse slope of the feature. Capt. Randle immediately appreciated that this particular bunker covered not only the rear of his new position but also the line of communication of the Battalion and therefore the destruction of the enemy post was imperative if the operation was to succeed.

With utter disregard of the obvious danger to himself, Capt. Randle charged the Japanese machine gun post single-handed with a rifle and bayonet. Although bleeding in the face and mortally wounded by numerous bursts of machine gun fire, he reached the bunker and silenced the gun with a grenade thrown through the bunker slit. He then flung his body across the slit so that the aperture should be completely sealed.

The bravery shown by this officer could not have been surpassed and by his self-sacrifice he saved the lives of many of his men and enabled not only his own Company but the whole Battalion to gain its objective and win a decisive victory over the enemy.

(*The London Gazette*, 20th December 1944)

This remarkable action, resulting in one of twenty-seven Victoria Crosses awarded for the Burma front, is regarded by many as the most heroic Victoria Cross act of the Second World War.

The Victoria Cross and medal group of Private/Corporal R. H. Burton, Duke of Wellington's (West Riding) Regiment (1923–93). An award for the fighting at Monte Ceco, Italy, 8th–9th October 1944, his VC is shown here with his other medals for 1939–45 and the 1953 Coronation Medal.

Fighting in central Italy, 1944–5. The hard-fought campaign to wrest control of the Italian peninsula – fighting dominated by mountain ranges and difficult river crossings – led to the award of twenty Victoria Crosses to British and Imperial forces.

PRIVATE RICHARD H. BURTON, 1ST DUKE OF WELLINGTON'S REGIMENT

In Italy on 8th October 1944, two companies of the Duke of Wellington's Regiment moved forward to take a strongly held feature 760 metres high. The capture of this feature was vital at this stage of the operations as it dominated all the main ground on the axis of the advance. The assaulting troops made good progress to within 20 yards of the crest where they came under withering fire from Spandaus on the crest. The leading Platoon was held up and the Platoon Commander wounded. The Company Commander took another Platoon, of which Private Burton was a runner, through to assault the crest from which four Spandaus were firing. Pte. Burton rushed forward and, engaging the first Spandau position with his Tommy Gun, killed the crew of three. When the assault was again held up by murderous fire from two more machine-guns, Pte. Burton, again showing complete disregard for his own safety, dashed forward towards the first machine gun using his Tommy Gun until his ammunition was exhausted. He then picked up a Bren Gun and firing from the hip succeeded in killing or wounding the crews of the two machine guns. Thanks to his outstanding courage the Company was then able to consolidate on the forward slope of the feature. The enemy immediately counter-attacked fiercely but Pte. Burton, in spite of most of his comrades being either dead or wounded, once again dashed forward on his own initiative and directed such accurate fire with his Bren Gun on the enemy that they retired leaving the feature firmly in our hands. The enemy later attacked again on an adjoining Platoon position and Pte. Burton, who had

Crossing the Senio River, Italy, early in April 1945. The later stages of the fighting in Italy involved complex operations across many wide and heavily defended rivers. The 8th Army's attempt to force the Argenta Gap via the Senio led to the award of two Victoria Crosses to Indian soldiers – Sepoy Ali Haidar (1913–99) of the 6–13th Rifles and Havildar Namdeo Jadhao (1921–84) of the 5th Mahratta Light Infantry.

Field Marshal Lord Wavell, Viceroy of India, presents the posthumous Victoria Cross to the widow of Rifleman Sherbahadur Thapa (1921–44), 1–9th Gurkhas. His award was for the fighting in San Marino, Italy, on 19th September 1944. The personal presentation by the Viceroy is in keeping with the intention to award the Victoria Cross under the most prestigious and formal of circumstances where possible.

Drawing by Bryan de Grineau for 'The Illustrated London News' showing Sergeant George Eardley's Victoria Cross action on 16th October 1944. Eardley successively destroyed three German machine-gun positions in orchards near Overloon, thus enabling the advance to continue.

placed himself on the flank, brought such accurate fire to bear that this counter-attack also failed to dislodge the Company from its position. Pte. Burton's magnificent gallantry and total disregard of his own safety during many hours of fighting in mud and continuous rain were an inspiration to all his comrades.

(*The London Gazette*, 4th January 1945)

This magnificent citation represents one of twenty Victoria Crosses awarded for the hard-fought Italian campaign of 1943–5.

ACTING SERGEANT GEORGE HAROLD EARDLEY, 4TH KING'S SHROPSHIRE LIGHT INFANTRY

In N. W. Europe, on 16th October 1944, during an attack on the wooded area east of Overloon, strong opposition was met from well-sited defensive positions in orchards. The enemy were paratroops and well equipped with machine guns.

A Platoon of the King's Shropshire Light Infantry was ordered to clear these orchards and restore the momentum of the advance but was halted some 80

When circumstances did not allow presentation of the actual Victoria Cross it was common for recipients to receive just the ribbon – to wear until the Cross could be formally presented. In wartime this was often carried out by senior commanders 'in the field'. In this instance Field Marshal Montgomery pins on the ribbon of the Victoria Cross awarded to Sergeant George Eardley, MM (1912–91), 4th King's Shropshire Light Infantry, for his gallantry at Overloon in October 1944. Eardley received the Victoria Cross itself from the hands of the King at a later ceremony in London.

yards from its objective by automatic fire from enemy machine gun posts. The fire was so heavy that it appeared impossible for any man to expose himself and remain unscathed.

Notwithstanding this, Sgt. Eardley, who had spotted one machine gun post, moved forward, firing his Sten gun, and killed the occupants of the post with a grenade. A second machine gun post beyond the first immediately opened up, spraying the area with fire. Sgt. Eardley, who was in a most exposed position, at once charged over 30 yards of open ground and silenced the enemy gunners.

The attack was continued by the Platoon but was again held up by a third machine gun post, and a section sent in to dispose of it was beaten back, losing four casualties. Sgt. Eardley, ordering the section he was with to lie down, then crawled forward alone and silenced the occupants of the post with a grenade.

The destruction of these three machine gun posts single-handedly by Sgt. Eardley, carried out under fire so heavy it daunted those who were with him, enabled his Platoon to achieve its objective and in so doing, ensured the success of the whole attack.

His outstanding initiative and magnificent bravery were the admiration of all who saw his gallant action.

(*The London Gazette*, 2nd January 1945)

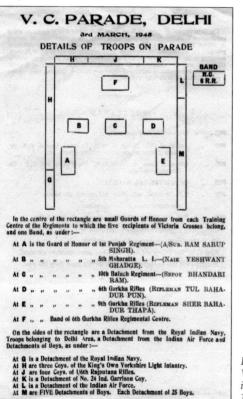

V. C. PARADE, DELHI
3rd MARCH, 1945
DETAILS OF TROOPS ON PARADE

In the centre of the rectangle are small Guards of Honour from each Training Centre of the Regiments to which the five recipients of Victoria Crosses belong, and one Band, as under :—

At **A** is the Guard of Honour of 1st Punjab Regiment—(A/Sub. RAM SARUP SINGH).
At **B** ,, ,, ,, ,, ,, ,, 5th Mahratta L. I.—(Naik YESHWANT GHADGE).
At **C** ,, ,, ,, ,, ,, ,, 10th Baluch Regiment—(Sepoy BHANDARI RAM).
At **D** ,, ,, ,, ,, ,, ,, 6th Gurkha Rifles (Rifleman TUL BAHA-DUR PUN).
At **E** ,, ,, ,, ,, ,, ,, 9th Gurkha Rifles (Rifleman SHER BAHA-DUR THAPA).
At **F** ,, ,, Band of 6th Gurkha Rifles Regimental Centre.

On the sides of the rectangle are a Detachment from the Royal Indian Navy, Troops belonging to Delhi Area, a Detachment from the Indian Air Force and Detachments of Boys, as under :—

At **G** is a Detachment of the Royal Indian Navy.
At **H** are three Coys. of the King's Own Yorkshire Light Infantry.
At **J** are four Coys. of 1/6th Rajputana Rifles.
At **K** is a Detachment of No. 24 Ind. Garrison Coy.
At **L** is a Detachment of the Indian Air Force.
At **M** are FIVE Detachments of Boys. Each Detachment of 25 Boys.

Programme for the Victoria Cross parade in Delhi, 31st March 1945.

The Korean War, 1951–3

In the first United Nations war, the British Army served as part of the UN force that came to the aid of South Korea following invasion by communist China. Four Victoria Crosses were awarded for this hard-fought campaign, of which two were posthumous.

PRIVATE WILLIAM SPEAKMAN, BLACK WATCH, ATTACHED TO 1ST KING'S OWN SCOTTISH BORDERERS

From 0400 hours, 4th November, 1951, the defensive positions held by 1st Battalion, The King's Own Scottish Borderers, were continuously subjected to heavy and accurate enemy shell and mortar fire. At 1545 hours, this fire became intense and continued thus for the next two hours, considerably damaging the defences and wounding a number of men. At 1645 hours, the enemy in their hundreds advanced in wave upon wave against the King's Own Scottish Borderers' positions, and by 1745 hours, fierce hand to hand fighting was taking place on every position.

Pte. Speakman, a member of B Company, Headquarters, learning that the section holding the left shoulder of the Company's position had been seriously depleted by casualties, had had its N.C.Os. wounded and was being overrun, decided on his own initiative to drive the enemy off the position and keep them off it. To effect this he collected quickly a large pile of grenades and a party of six men. Then displaying complete disregard for his own personal safety he led his party in a series of grenade charges against the enemy; and continued doing so as each successive wave of enemy reached the crest of the hill. The force and determination of his charges broke up each successive enemy onslaught and resulted in an ever mounting pile of enemy dead.

Having led some ten charges, through withering enemy machine gun and mortar fire, Pte. Speakman was eventually severely wounded in the leg. Undaunted by his wounds, he continued to lead charge after charge against the enemy and it was only after a direct order from his superior officer that he agreed to pause for a first field dressing to be applied to his wounds. Having had his wounds bandaged, Pte. Speakman immediately rejoined his comrades and led them again and again forward in a series of grenade charges, up to the time of the withdrawal of his Company at 2100 hours.

At the critical moment of the withdrawal, amidst an inferno of enemy machine gun and mortar fire, as well as grenades, Private Speakman led a final charge to clear the crest of the hill and hold it, whilst the remainder of his Company withdrew. Encouraging his gallant, but by now sadly depleted party, he assailed the enemy with showers of grenades and kept them at bay sufficiently long for his Company to effect its withdrawal.

Under the stress and strain of this battle, Private Speakman's outstanding powers of leadership were revealed and he so dominated the situation that he inspired his comrades to stand firm and fight the enemy to a standstill. His great gallantry and utter contempt for his own personal safety were an inspiration to all his comrades. He was, by his heroic actions, personally responsible for causing enormous losses to the enemy, assisting his Company to maintain their position for some four hours and saving the lives of many of his comrades when they were forced to withdraw from their position.

A British machine-gun in Korea, 1951. This three-year war, in which the United Nations fought China and North Korea, resulted in the award of four Victoria Crosses.

> Private Speakman's heroism under intense fire throughout the operation and when painfully wounded was beyond praise and is deserving of supreme recognition.
>
> (*The London Gazette*, 28th December 1951)

This Victoria Cross was conferred for the defence of Point 217, Korea, on 4th November 1951. Although his award was gazetted during the reign of King George VI, 'Bill' Speakman was the first VC to be invested by Queen Elizabeth II, the King having died in February 1952.

Later awards

Although British troops played no part in the Vietnam War, awards were made to Australian forces, since the Victoria Cross is open to Commonwealth countries. Four Victoria Crosses were granted to members of the Australian Army Training Team, Vietnam, for actions between 1965 and 1969. Two were posthumous.

Two awards of the Victoria Cross were made for the South Atlantic campaign of 1982 (the Falklands War). Both were posthumous and both went to the Parachute Regiment: to Lieutenant Colonel Herbert ('H') Jones (2nd Battalion) for gallantry

British 'Warrior' armoured fighting vehicles in Iraq, 2004, where Private Johnson Beharry's gallantry earned him a Victoria Cross.

at Goose Green and Darwin on 28th May 1982 and to Sergeant Ian McKay (3rd Battalion) for the attack on Mount Longdon, 11th–12th June 1982. The awards appeared in *The London Gazette* of 8th October 1982.

The latest award of the Victoria Cross at the time of publication was to Private Johnson Beharry, Princess of Wales's Royal Regiment, for conspicuous and selfless gallantry on two occasions in Iraq in the summer of 2004, when, although wounded, he rescued many colleagues under heavy fire.

The latest recipient of the Victoria Cross (at the time of publication), Private Johnson Beharry, Princess of Wales's Royal Regiment, who won the medal in Iraq in May 2004 for 'two individual acts of great heroism by which he saved the lives of his comrades. Both were in direct face of the enemy, under intense fire, at great personal risk to himself.' With his VC he wears the NATO medal for service in the Balkans and the Iraq campaign medal.

A Victoria Cross miscellany

The first awards

The earliest action to be rewarded with the Victoria Cross took place in the Baltic on 21st June 1854, when Mate Charles Lucas of HMS *Hecla* picked up and threw overboard a live shell, saving many lives. However, the first Victoria Cross award to be published in *The London Gazette* was that to Lieutenant Cecil W. Buckley, Royal Navy, who received the Cross for his gallantry in the Sea of Azoff on 29th May and 3rd June 1855 when landing to destroy Russian stores near Genitchi and Taganrog. Lieutenant Henry Raby, Royal Navy, decorated for bravery at the storming of the Redan at Sebastopol on 18th June 1855, became the first man actually to be presented with the Victoria Cross when he was the first of sixty-two recipients to receive the award from the hands of Queen Victoria at the ceremony in Hyde Park on 26th June 1857.

Number of awards for one action

The greatest number of awards made for one day's fighting is twenty-four, for the fighting in Lucknow on 16th November 1857 during the Indian Mutiny. The largest number for one distinct action is eleven, for the defence of Rorke's Drift on 22nd–23rd January 1879 during the Zulu War. In Gallipoli on 25th April 1915 the 1st Lancashire Fusiliers earned their famous 'six VCs before breakfast' in the bloody landings at 'W' Beach, Cape Helles, which cost the battalion 360 casualties.

The first Victoria Cross incident: Mate Charles Lucas of HMS Hecla throws overboard a burning shell that had landed on the deck, thus saving many lives. This occurred on 21st June 1854 during the Baltic Campaign – part of the larger Russian War of 1854–6. Lucas (1834–1914) ended his career as a Rear Admiral.

Gallipoli landings: the 'River Clyde' disgorges two thousand men on to 'V' Beach at Cape Helles on 25th April 1915. Six Victoria Crosses were awarded to naval officers and ratings from the 'River Clyde' for gallantry during the fiercely contested and costly landings at this point.

Perhaps surprisingly, some famous military operations have produced comparatively few Victoria Crosses. The large-scale operations involved in the defence and relief of Chitral on the North West Frontier of India in 1895 produced only one award, as did the expedition to Tibet in 1903–4 and the extensive anti-terrorist operations in Malaysia from 1963 to 1966. Also, as mentioned earlier, there was only one award for air combat over the United Kingdom during the Battle of Britain and, remarkably under the circumstances, there was only one for the landings on D-Day, 6th June 1944 – that to Company Sergeant Major Stanley Hollis, 6th Green Howards (1912–72).

Double awards

Only three men have received a bar to the Victoria Cross (that is, two Victoria Crosses). Surgeon Major Arthur Martin-Leake (1874–1953) was awarded a Victoria Cross for tending the wounded under heavy fire at Vlakfontein on 8th February 1902 during the Second Boer War and went on to earn a bar to the Victoria Cross at

An early First World War portrait, on a cigarette card, of Surgeon Major Martin-Leake, Royal Army Medical Corps, the first winner of two Victoria Crosses.

A replica of the Victoria Cross with a second award bar.

Zonnebeke in Belgium in November 1914 for similar devotion to the wounded under fire. Captain Noel Chavasse (1884–1917), Royal Army Medical Corps, earned the Victoria Cross and the bar for gallantry in France in 1916 and in Belgium in 1917; unfortunately he died of wounds received during his second Victoria Cross action. The last 'double VC' was the New Zealander Captain Charles Upham (1908–94), who received the Victoria Cross for gallantry at Maleme in Crete in May 1941 and the bar for gallantry at El Ruweisat Ridge in the Western Desert of Egypt in July 1942.

Youngest and oldest

The youngest recipients of the Victoria Cross were Drummer Thomas Flinn, 64th Regiment (1842–92), and Hospital

Captain Charles Upham, the New Zealander who was the only recipient of the Victoria Cross and bar in the Second World War.

The grave of Captain Noel Chavasse, VC, MC. One of only three winners of the Victoria Cross with bar, he is buried at Brandhoek near Ypres. His tombstone carries two representations of the Victoria Cross.

Boy 1st Class John Cornwell (1900–16), mortally wounded early in the action, remains alone at his gun position on HMS Chester during the greatest sea battle of the 1914–18 war at Jutland, 31st May 1916. Cornwell, at sixteen years and four months old, was one of the youngest recorded recipients of the Victoria Cross. Four Crosses were conferred for the battle, two of them posthumously.

Apprentice Andrew Fitzgibbon, Indian Medical Establishment attached to the 67th Regiment (1845–83). The former won the award for his gallantry at Cawnpore in 1857 during the Indian Mutiny and the latter during the assault on the Taku Forts in China in 1860, when he attended the wounded under heavy fire. Both were aged only fifteen years and three months at the time of the action. Perhaps the most famous of the 'young VCs' is Boy 1st Class John Cornwell, who was sixteen years and four months old when, during the Battle of Jutland (31st May 1916), he remained at his gun position on HMS *Chester* although mortally wounded.

There is some dispute over the oldest recipient of the Victoria Cross, but it is generally accepted to be Lieutenant William Raynor of the Bengal Veteran Establishment, who was one of three men awarded the Victoria Cross for the defence of the Magazine at Delhi in May 1857. He was then aged sixty-one years and ten months. He died in India in 1860.

Not in action

Although universally considered as an award for bravery in action, there have been instances in which the Victoria Cross was conferred for actions not before the enemy. The most notable of these occurred in May 1867, when a group of soldiers of the 24th Regiment volunteered to take a boat across dangerous surf to rescue men trapped on a beach on Little Andaman Island in the

A Victorian replica VC named to and probably worn by Sergeant Timothy O'Hea, one of the few men to have received the VC for an incident not 'before the enemy'. O'Hea put out a fire in an ammunition train near Danville, Quebec, on 9th June 1866.

Bay of Bengal. All five volunteers were awarded the Victoria Cross. Another example is that of Private T. O'Hea (1843–74) of The Rifle Brigade, who was awarded the Victoria Cross in 1866 for putting out a fire in a train carriage loaded with ammunition in Quebec. The award of the Victoria Cross under such circumstances did not find favour with sections of the War Office and was effectively ended by a change to the regulations in 1881, which directed that the medal should be won for actions only 'in the presence of the enemy'. The introduction of a wider range of gallantry medals in later times (for example the Albert Medal, the Empire Gallantry Medal and the George Cross) did allow bravery in other circumstances to receive official reward.

Family awards

Interestingly, there have been a number of instances of awards to members of the same family.

Four pairs of brothers have won the Victoria Cross:

Lieutenant Colonel Roland Bradford, Military Cross, 9th Durham Light Infantry (France, 1st October 1916) and Lieutenant Commander George Bradford, Royal Navy (posthumous, Zeebrugge, 23rd April 1918).

Major Charles Gough, 5th Bengal European Cavalry (Indian Mutiny, 15th August 1857) and Lieutenant Hugh Gough, 1st Bengal European Light Cavalry (Indian Mutiny, 12th November 1857 and 25th February 1858) (Charles Gough's son – Hugh Gough's nephew – Major J. E. Gough also won the Victoria Cross, in Somaliland on 22nd April 1903).

Lieutenant the Honourable F. H. S. Roberts, King's Royal Rifle Corps. Son of Lord Roberts, VC, he was awarded the Cross for his part in the attempt to save the guns at Colenso in 1899 (see page 29). Roberts died of his wounds two days after the action and there was some doubt expressed at the time as to whether he should receive the medal, since posthumous awards were not conferred at that time.

Major William La Touche Congreve, Rifle Brigade (1891–1916). He was awarded the Victoria Cross for conspicuous gallantry on the Western Front over a period of fourteen days of severe fighting on the Somme in July 1916. Congreve, who was killed in action near Longueval on 20th July 1916, had also received the Distinguished Service Order, the Military Cross and the Legion of Honour. His father, Captain Walter Congreve, Rifle Brigade (1862–1927), had won the Victoria Cross at Colenso in South Africa in December 1899. (Portrait by J. St H. Lander)

Major Reginald Sartorius, 6th Bengal Cavalry (Ashantee War, 17th January 1874) and Captain Euston Sartorius, 59th Regiment (Afghan War, 24th October 1879).

Second-Lieutenant Alexander Turner, 1st Berkshire Regiment (France, 28th September 1915) and Lieutenant Colonel Victor Turner, Rifle Brigade (Western Desert, Egypt, 27th October 1942).

Three father-and-son pairs have received the Victoria Cross:

Lieutenant (later Field Marshal Lord) Frederick S. Roberts, Bengal Horse Artillery (Indian Mutiny, 2nd January 1858) and his son Lieutenant F. H. S. Roberts, King's Royal Rifle Corps (Second Boer War, 15th December 1899).

Captain Walter Congreve, Rifle Brigade (Second Boer War, 15th December 1899) and his son Major William Congreve, Rifle Brigade (France, 6th–20th July 1916).

Charles Gough and his son John (see opposite).

There have also been examples of in-laws and cousins winning the Victoria Cross.

Warfare over England: Lieutenant William Leefe Robinson (1895–1918) was awarded the first Victoria Cross for an action over English soil. Using a new type of incendiary bullet, he brought down the German army airship SL-11 over Cuffley in Hertfordshire on the night of 2nd/3rd September 1916. SL-11 was one of a fleet of sixteen army airships and Zeppelins that attacked London that night. Robinson, who was taken prisoner in 1917, died in the influenza epidemic in 1918.

Awards in the United Kingdom

Only three awards of the Victoria Cross have been made for service within the bounds of the United Kingdom. The first was to Captain W. L. Robinson (1895–1918) of the Worcester Regiment and Royal Flying Corps, who attacked and brought down a German airship over Cuffley, Hertfordshire, on 3rd September 1916. This was the first 'Zeppelin' to be destroyed over the United Kingdom. The second was awarded posthumously to Leading Seaman J. F. Mantle, Royal Navy (1917–40), for gallantry during an air attack on his ship, HMS *Foylebank*, in Portland harbour on 4th July 1940. The last was that conferred upon Flight Lieutenant E. J. B. Nicolson, Royal Air Force (1917–45), for gallantry in air combat over Southampton on 16th August 1940.

Civilian awards

The issue of civilian eligibility for the Victoria Cross proved a thorny subject when first broached during the Indian Mutiny of 1857–8. In the event, four Crosses were awarded to civilians during the campaign – to Ross Mangles, W. F. McDonell and Thomas Henry Kavanagh, all members of the Bengal Civil Service, and to G. B. Chicken, a civilian volunteer serving with the Naval Brigade. Kavanagh is an interesting example. Having served in the Defence

A civilian VC: Thomas Henry Kavanagh (1821–82), Bengal Civil Service, being disguised before his mission to cross enemy lines in Lucknow and guide the relief force into the city, 9th November 1857.

of Lucknow, he volunteered to disguise himself as an Indian to pass through enemy siege lines and through the city itself to reach the approaching relief column so that he could guide them towards the besieged Residency. Needless to say, it was an exceptionally dangerous mission, but he succeeded in his goal. Technically, the last civilian recipient was the Reverend James W. Adams, awarded the Victoria Cross during the Second Afghan War (1878–80) for going under close fire to the assistance of fallen cavalrymen during the action at Kili Kazi near Kabul on 11th December 1879. However, an amendment of the Victoria Cross Warrant in 1881, before Adams's award was gazetted, extended the award to priests of the Indian Ecclesiastical Departments when they were serving with the army in the field, so Adams is usually classed as a military recipient.

Awards to foreigners

The Warrant of the Victoria Cross made no specific allowance for the award of the medal to people who were not subjects of the British monarch. Nevertheless, a number have been awarded to foreign nationals – five Americans, one Belgian, two Germans, three Danes, one Swiss, one Swede and one Russian. Ferdinand Schiess (1856–84), a Swiss national serving with the Natal Native Contingent, was awarded the Victoria Cross during the Zulu War for gallantry during the defence of Rorke's Drift, January 22nd–23rd 1879; he was also the first man serving with a South

African unit to receive the award. The Dane Anders Lassen (1920–45) was awarded the Victoria Cross for a raid in which he was mortally wounded on Lake Comacchio in Italy in April 1945. He had already won the Military Cross and two bars.

It is interesting to note that the American Unknown Warrior of the 1914–18 war buried at Arlington National Cemetery was awarded a posthumous Victoria Cross while the British Unknown Soldier, interred in Westminster Abbey, was not. He was, however, awarded the Congressional Medal of Honor by the United States government.

Awards to women

The original Warrant made no reference to the possibility or otherwise of awards to women but no woman has received the Victoria Cross. Perhaps the nearest candidate was Mrs Webber Harris, wife of the Commanding Officer of the 104th Bengal Fusiliers, who displayed outstanding courage and devotion in nursing the men of the regiment during a cholera epidemic in India in September 1859. She was presented with a gold replica of the Victoria Cross (without its 'For Valour' legend) by the officers of the 104th as a token of appreciation. This was entirely unofficial, though it was presented to her personally by General Sir Sam Browne, VC.

Awards by ballot

The regulations of the Victoria Cross contain a rather unusual term. Rule 13 directed that in circumstances in which a large

Mrs Webber Harris, presented with a gold replica Victoria Cross for her untiring attentions while nursing the victims of a cholera outbreak in the 104th Bengal Fusiliers in India in 1859. Although no woman has been awarded the actual Victoria Cross, many have received other gallantry awards.

Major E. J. Phipps-Hornby (1857–1947) was awarded the Victoria Cross for his gallantry in saving the guns of his battery, 'Q' Royal Horse Artillery, at Sannah's Post (or Korn Spruit) in South Africa on 31st March 1900. His was one of five Victoria Crosses granted for the action, three of which were awarded by ballot.

number of men (for example a Royal Air Force squadron, a ship's crew or a battalion) had displayed conspicuous gallantry in an action, so that it was not easy to identify possible individual recipients, the men involved could choose a recipient or recipients from among their own ranks. This clause has been invoked on a number of famous occasions, some examples being: the four awards to the 53rd Shropshire Regiment for their attack on the Secunderabagh at Lucknow in May 1857; the 'six VCs before breakfast' to the 1st Lancashire Fusiliers for the Gallipoli Landings in 1915 and to some of the naval forces engaged in the Zeebrugge Raid in April 1918. It seems reasonable enough for the men who were there and saw what happened to select from among themselves the recipients of a limited number of Victoria Crosses, but this democratic element is unheard of for any other gallantry award.

Posthumous awards

Initially there was no facility to award the Victoria Cross posthumously. The most that could be done was to record a 'mention in dispatches' and to affirm that 'had he survived, he would have been recommended for the award of the Victoria Cross'. Since so many acts of outstanding gallantry had actually resulted in the death of the performer, this was clearly an anomaly requiring reform. King Edward VII – a monarch who took a real interest in decorations and medals – began the practice of awarding retrospective, posthumous Victoria Crosses in 1902, and a

Gravestones set up by the Commonwealth War Graves Commission for Victoria Cross winners always depict the Cross itself, in addition to the usual details. Shown here is the grave of Private R. Morrow of the Royal Irish Rifles, at White House Cemetery near Ypres. He was killed on 26th April 1915, two weeks after his Victoria Cross action in which he had rescued many injured men under heavy fire.

number were then given to the next-of-kin of deceased recipients. Perhaps the most famous of these awards were those to Lieutenants Melville and Coghill, 24th Foot, who were killed in an attempt to save their Regimental Colours at Isandhlwana during the Zulu War. However, formal recognition of the practice in the form of an amendment to the Regulations did not come until 1920, following the experience of the 1914–18 war. Nearly three hundred Victoria Crosses have been granted posthumously – slightly less than a quarter of the total number of awards.

Forfeitures

As with other high-ranking decorations and honours, the original Warrant of the Victoria Cross allowed that a recipient could forfeit the medal if he was convicted of a criminal offence, civil or military, that might be deemed to bring the award into disrepute. This involved handing back the medal, having one's name erased from the Register of recipients and losing the Victoria Cross pension. It goes without saying that such a forfeiture was regarded as a deep disgrace.

In the first fifty years of its existence eight Victoria Crosses were forfeited. The crimes leading to forfeiture were varied and included theft and desertion, but one example may suffice. Gunner James Collis (1856–1918), of E-B, Royal Horse Artillery, was

Obverse and reverse of a modern copy Victoria Cross. Many different types are commercially available and their quality and accuracy of detail varies considerably.

awarded the Victoria Cross for conspicuous gallantry in the attempt to save the guns of his battery from falling into enemy hands at the disastrous battle of Maiwand in Afghanistan in August 1880. Some years later he was convicted of bigamy and was accordingly required to return his Victoria Cross and see his name erased from the Register. Collis went on to serve in the First World War and after his death in 1918 his family petitioned the King to allow his name to be re-entered on the Register of Victoria Cross winners. King George V took a serious interest in the case and as a direct result the regulation allowing for forfeiture was amended in 1920 and no recipient of the Victoria Cross has since forfeited the award. The King summed up the situation very forcibly: 'Even were a VC to be sentenced to be hanged for murder, he should be allowed to wear his Victoria Cross on the scaffold.' The names of the eight forfeited Victoria Cross recipients were subsequently restored to the Register.

Duplicates and replacements

By custom, recipients who have lost their Victoria Cross are able to claim an official replacement and have to pay the cost of a duplicate (though they are not marked as such), manufactured by

A contemporary replica Victoria Cross. This one was worn by Private Samuel Parkes, 4th Light Dragoons, who won the award for gallantry during the Charge of the Light Brigade on 25th October 1854. Parkes subsequently lost his original Victoria Cross and wore this replica, which for many years was displayed in the collection of the United Services' Institute in London. It is now in a private collection.

A replica Victoria Cross by Hancocks of London, who have made the Cross since its inception. These high-quality replicas are produced for museum display and are closer to the originals in look and dimensions than other commercially available copies of the award.

Hancocks. They can, of course, buy for themselves any commercially made version and it is well known that many Victoria Cross recipients wear a replica rather than risk losing the real item. In early times, some recipients who fell on hard times are known to have sold their Cross. This was frowned upon by the authorities – and was illegal for personnel still serving – and one aim of the annuity to recipients (see below) was to prevent this happening once they had left the services. We should also remember that there have always been collectors willing to pay temptingly high prices for examples of the medal. A sold Victoria Cross could not be officially replaced and it is likely that some recipients who sold their Cross later claimed it as 'lost' and applied for an official replacement or at least bought themselves a private-purchase type.

Pensions

When originally instituted, the Victoria Cross carried a special pension of £10 per annum to non-commissioned ranks (who would continue to receive it if later commissioned). From 1898 this could be increased in cases of real need to up to £50, at the discretion of the authorities, and later the discretionary limit was raised to £75. Officers were allowed the gratuity from 1920 onwards. These

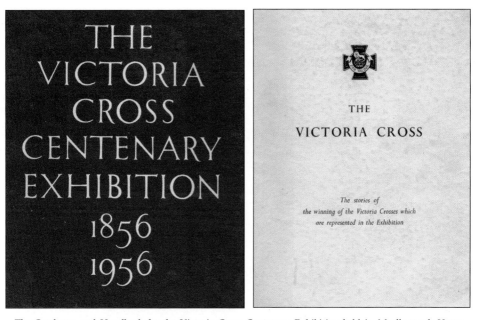

The Catalogue and Handbook for the Victoria Cross Centenary Exhibition held in Marlborough House, June–July 1956. This event housed the largest collection of Victoria Crosses and related material ever put on public display.

figures remained in force until as late as 1959, when the gratuity was increased to £100 per annum, payable to all recipients as a lump sum regardless of rank or need. Not until 1995 was this increased to the more respectable but hardly generous figure of £1300. Thirty-three winners were then alive to receive the new payment. At the time of publication thirteen recipients are still alive.

The Centenary Exhibition 1956 and The Victoria Cross Association

In 1956, on the centenary of the institution of the Victoria Cross, a major exhibition was mounted at Marlborough House, running from 15th June to 28th July. It brought together the largest selection of Victoria Crosses, Victoria Cross groups, portraits and ephemera ever assembled, borrowing items from recipients' families, private collectors, regiments and museums all over the world. At that time, some four hundred recipients were still alive.

During the celebrations, Brigadier Sir John Smyth, Bt, VC, MC, MP, was asked to establish a formal society for holders of the Victoria Cross. The result was the establishment of The Victoria Cross Association, based in St George's House, London, under the aegis of the Royal Society. Its inaugural meeting assembled in Westminster Hall on 25th June 1956 and on the morning of 27th

Recipients of the Victoria Cross have always been honoured guests at regimental reunions and ceremonies. Here, former Sergeant Harold Whitfield, VC, of the Shropshire Yeomanry (see page 25), and former Sergeant George Eardley, VC, MM, of the 4th King's Shropshire Light Infantry (see page 47), attend a reunion in Copthorne Barracks, Shrewsbury, in 1956.

June the new association met as such at St George's House with twenty-four VCs, thirteen from the United Kingdom and eleven from the Commonwealth. At the second meeting, in 1960, George Cross holders were offered associate membership and in 1962, at the third reunion, a decision was made to grant holders of the George Cross full membership. As a result the association was renamed the 'Victoria Cross and George Cross Association'. It meets in London every two or three years.

Further reading

All awards of the Victoria Cross are published in *The London Gazette*, many appearing in its supplements, and editions are to be found in major libraries. Original correspondence and recommendations are held in the Royal Archives at Windsor and in the National Archives at Kew in series WO.98 and WO.32 and others.

There is a large and growing list of reference and general works on the Victoria Cross, some specific to campaigns or regiments or even to individual recipients – indeed, no British honour or medal has attracted such a large range of printed works and, as books continue to appear with great regularity, there is no sign of that interest waning. The very best account of the origins of the Victoria Cross and changes to its regulations is *The Evolution of the Victoria Cross* by M. J. Crook (Midas Books, 1975); good general registers and catalogues are *The Register of the Victoria Cross* ('This England' Books, 1988) and the detailed *The Victoria Cross 1856–1920* by Sir O'Moore Creagh and E. M. Humphries (originally printed in 1926, reprinted by Hayward in 1978).

Many early works on the Victoria Cross tend to be of less value today. Some late Victorian 'popular' works, such as *The Victoria Cross in Zululand* (Major W. J. Elliott, Dean & Son, London, 1880), or books from the time of the 1914–18 war, tend to emphasise tales of derring-do and are little more than historical curiosities. Exceptions are *The Book of the VC* by A. L. Haydon (Melrose, 1906), *The VC: Its Heroes and Their Valour* by D. H. Parry (London, 1913) and *The Victoria Cross* by R. Stewart (Hutchinson, 1928). *The Bronze Cross: A Tribute to Those Who Won the Supreme Award for Valour in the Years 1940–45* by F. G. Roe, published at the end of the Second World War (Gawthorn, 1945), is also of value.

The grave of James Langley Dalton, VC (1832–87), in Russell Road Catholic Cemetery, Port Elizabeth, South Africa. Although great efforts are being made to locate and repair the graves of Victoria Cross winners, some – such as this, to one of the heroes of Rorke's Drift – are poorly maintained and at risk.

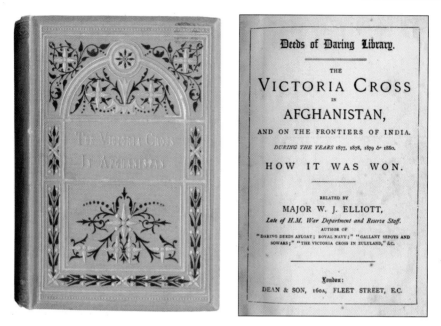

Many early books on the Victoria Cross tend to concentrate on the 'Boy's Own' aspect of the actions.

What follows is only a small selection of more general works, chosen from a large range now available; for a detailed bibliography, consult J. Mulholland and A. Jordan (editors), *Victoria Cross Bibliography* (Spink, 1999).

Arthur, M. *Symbol of Courage: A Complete History of the Victoria Cross.* Sidgwick & Jackson, 2003.

Bancroft, J. W. *Local Heroes: Boer War VCs.* The House of Heroes, 2003.

Batchelor, P. F., and Matson, C. *VCs of the First World War: The Western Front 1915.* Wrens Park Publishing, 1999.

Biggs, M. *The Story of Gurkha VCs.* Gurkha Museum, 1993.

Bowyer, C. *The Air VCs.* Kimber, 1978.

Cooksley, P. G. *VCs of the First World War: the Air VCs.* Wrens Park Publishing, 1999.

Doherty, R., and Truesdale, D. *Irish Winners of the VC.* Courts Press, 2000.

Gliddon, G. *VCs of the First World War: 1914.* Budding Books, 1997.

Gliddon, G. *VCs of the First World War: the Somme.* Budding Books, 1997.

Gliddon, G. *VCs of the First World War: the Spring Offensive 1918.* Sutton Publishing, 1997.

Gliddon, G. *VCs of the First World War: Arras and Messines 1917.* Wrens Park Publishing, 2000.

Gliddon, G. *VCs of the First World War: The Final Days 1918.* Sutton Publishing, 2000.

Gliddon, G. *VCs of the First World War: The Road to Victory 1918.* Sutton Publishing, 2000.

HMSO. *VC Centenary Exhibition: Catalogues.* 1956.

Johns, W. E., *The Air VCs.* Hamilton, 1935.

Kempton, C. *Valour and Gallantry: HEIC and Indian Army VCs and GCs 1856–1946.* The Military Press, 2001.

Laffin, J. *British VCs of World War Two: A Study in Heroism.* Budding Books, 2000.

Little, M. G. *The Royal Marines VCs*. Royal Marines Museum, undated.

Napier, G. *The Sapper VCs*. HMSO, 1999.

National Army Museum. *The VCs and GCs of the Honourable East India Company and Indian Army, 1856–1945*. 1962.

Smyth, Sir John. *The Story of the VC, 1856–1963*. Muller, 1963.

Snelling, S. *VCs of the First World War: Gallipoli*. Wrens Park Publishing, 1999.

Snelling, S. *VCs of the First World War: Passchendaele*. Sutton Park Publishing, 1998.

Swettenham, H. *Valiant Men: Canada's VC and GC Winners*. Hakkert, 1973.

Turner, J. F. *VCs of the Royal Navy*. George Harrap, 1956.

Turner, J. F. *VCs of the Air*. George Harrap, 1961; reprinted by Wrens Park Publishing, 2001.

Turner, J. F. *VCs of the Army 1939–51*. George Harrap, 1962.

Uys, I. S. *For Valour: The History of South Africa's VC Heroes*. Uys, 1973.

Uys, I. S. *VCs of the Anglo-Boer War*. Uys, 2000.

Victoria Cross Society. *Journal*.

Wigmore, L., and Harding, B. *They Dared Mightily*. Australian War Memorial, 1973.

Williams, W. A. *The VCs of Wales and the Welsh Regiments*. Bridge Books, 1984.

Winton, J. *The VC at Sea*. M. Joseph, 1978.

A great deal of work is being done to record and research Victoria Cross recipients and to identify or restore their graves and memorials. An interesting addition to the library in this respect is *Monuments to Courage: VC Headstones and Memorials* by D. Harvey (two volumes, K. and K. Patience, 1999; reprinted by The Naval and Military Press, 1999).

The Victoria Cross group of Trumpet Major Robert Kells, 9th Lancers. He won his VC in India in September 1857 for defending a wounded officer under close fire and carrying him to safety. He also has the medal for the Punjab campaign (1848–9), the Indian Mutiny medal with three clasps and the Long Service and Good Conduct Medal. Kells (1832–1905) later became a Yeoman of the Guard.

Places to visit

The largest collection of Victoria Crosses and associated groups is displayed in the Victoria Cross and George Cross Gallery of the Imperial War Museum, Lambeth Road, London. A selection of large military and naval museums that include good displays of the Victoria Cross is given below. Local regimental and military museums are also worth a visit. As there are some 150 in Britain, consult *A Guide to Military Museums* by T. and S. Wise (Imperial Press, Knighton) for details of collections and opening hours.

'Firepower', The Museum of the Royal Artillery, The Royal Arsenal, Woolwich, London SE18 6ST. Telephone: 020 8855 7755. Website: www.firepower.org.uk

Gurkha Museum, Peninsula Barracks, Romsey Road, Winchester, Hampshire SO23 8TS. Telephone: 01962 842832. Website: www.thegurkhamuseum.co.uk

Imperial War Museum, Lambeth Road, London SE1 6HZ. Telephone: 020 7416 5000. Website: http://london.iwm.org.uk

Museum of Army Flying, Middle Wallop, Stockbridge, Hampshire SO20 8DY. Telephone: 01264 784421. Website: www.flying-museum.org.uk

The National Army Museum, Royal Hospital Road, Chelsea, London SW3 4HT. Telephone: 020 7730 0717 (switchboard). Website: www.national-army-museum.ac.uk

The RAF Museum, Grahame Park Way, Hendon, London NW9 5LL. Telephone: 020 8205 2266. Website: www.rafmuseum.org.uk

The Royal Marines Museum, Southsea, Hampshire PO4 9PX. Telephone: 023 9281 9385. Website: www.royalmarinesmuseum.co.uk

The Royal Naval Museum, The Historic Dockyard, Portsmouth PO1 3NU. Telephone: 023 9272 7562. Website: www.royalnavalmuseum.org

The Tank Museum, Bovington Camp, Dorset BH20 6JG. Telephone: 01929 405096. Website: www.tankmuseum.org

The Illustrated London News features the award of 'the new order of valour' – with the original blue ribbon for the Navy – in its issue of 20th June 1857.

Other useful information

Leading auctioneers

Examples of the Victoria Cross occasionally come up for sale. For those wishing to purchase a Victoria Cross or related miniatures and ephemera, the leading auctioneers listed below handle such valuable and rare items.

Dix, Noonan, Webb, 16 Bolton Street, London W1J 8BQ. Telephone: 020 7016 1700. Website: www.dnw.co.uk

Morton & Eden, 45 Maddox Street, London W1S 2PE. Telephone: 020 7493 5344. Website: www.mortonandeden.com

Spink & Son, 69 Southampton Row, Bloomsbury, London WC1B 4ET. Telephone: 020 7563 4000. Website: www.spink-online.com

Websites

The Internet offers many good reference sites and a search using 'Victoria Cross' or simply the name of a recipient will produce a wide range of sites. Among the best are www.victoriacrosssociety.com, www.victoriacross.org.uk and www.victoriacross.net

Society

The Victoria Cross Society is a specialist association set up by enthusiasts and historians to study and publicise the award and issues regular journals. For details contact the Secretary (Kintons, Harlequin Place, Crowborough, East Sussex TN6 1HZ. Telephone: 01892 664234. Email: secretary@victoriacrosssociety.com) or consult the website (www.victoriacrosssociety.com).

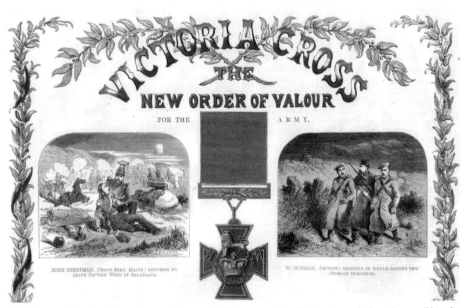

The Illustrated London News features the award of 'the new order of valour' – with the crimson ribbon for the Army – in its issue of 20th June 1857.

Index